Edited by:
Hettie Davies and Anne Llewelyn

Published by The Bynea & Llwynhendy History Group
Copyright © 2010

Design: Clive Davies Design

Printed by Harcourt Litho
Swansea

ISBN: 978-0-9566920-0-9

Cover Photography by Mr. Roger Jones

Photograph on back cover
The trolley bus terminus at the Plough Inn
– Bynea (note the trolley bus wires)

Reminiscences Past to Present

Atgofion Gorffennol i'r Presennol

A Journey through Bynea and Llwynhendy

Taith drwy Bynea a Llwynhendy

Contents

Acknowledgements

The Bynea and Llwynhendy History Society would like to thank everyone for helping in preparing and putting together this second book of our district's history. It is difficult to mention names as so many have contributed and the fear we have is that we would leave someone out.

However we would like to thank all of you who has made it possible for us to print this book. As you can see the book is full of old and new photographs and thank you all for allowing us to use your precious photographs, also those of you that have written articles for us, as without them it would have been impossible to put this book together.

We thank those that have read over the work before going to print, to make sure that all the facts, and of course, the spellings were correct.

However there are a few that we must mention by name.

We would like to thank all those that have helped us financially, Rees Electrical Repairs, Huntsman, and Schaffler.

To our designer, Mr Clive Davies for his endless patience, whilst guiding us through the world of book producing.

The book includes some Welsh articles and we would like to thank Mrs Helen Lane (nee Roberts) for her help in translating them so that our non Welsh speakers can also enjoy our book.

The Reference Library have been a great help to us, helping to provide the required article or newspaper. It is thanks to them that we were able to produce the map on our cover.

Also thank you to Catrin Llewelyn who gave us technical guidance, and Alison Howell with the typing.

Last, but by far not least, we would like to thank Mr. Terry Davies, who has constantly encouraged and helped us to achieve our goal.

We hope that we have not left anyone out, and if we have, please accept our sincere apology. In the event of any errors, we assume responsibility, but hope there aren't too many.

We hope that you will enjoy reading and browsing over the photographs, and that you will get as much pleasure in doing so as we have had in putting it together.

Gobeithiwn y mwynhewch ddarllen ac edrych trwy'r llyfr hyn.

Diolch yn fawr   Thank you
Hettie a Anne   Hettie & Anne

Introduction

"You can take a person out of Bynea, but you cannot take Bynea out of the person". This dictum is certainly true of our village and is reflected in the meetings that we have as the Bynea and Llwynhendy History group at the Red Cow. Reminiscences flow and members are enthused as they relate various anecdotes and recollections of the village. Bynea was without doubt a true village, founded on heavy industry and having a strong cultural tradition. There were many shops selling a whole range of products and services, but the one that is embedded in my memory is Maggie's Chip Shop with its sawdust covered floor and benches where we all sat in eager anticipation of glorious rissole and chips.

Time has removed places such as the park, the village hall and old Bynea school, but they have been replaced by new institutions such as Saron Hall and the impressive new school.

The first book published in the year 2000 was a comprehensive history of Bynea and Llwynhendy and was a great success. The present volume is less detailed with an emphasis on the pictorial record. The theme of the book is a journey through the village from an entry point being new Loughor Bridge and culminating in Llwynhendy. It contains excellent photographs and records of events and situations as the perambulation is made through the village.

All members of the History group have been involved but credit must be given to two "guiding lights," - Mrs Hettie Davies and Mrs Anne Llewelyn (nee Dykes) who have worked tirelessly to collate information and prepare it for publication.

I hope you enjoy reading this book and be tempted to visit and wander around our interesting village.

Rowland S. Evans.

Rowland Evans *(Chairman)*
June 2010

Sera

Merch ei milltir sgwâr oedd Sera. Roedd hi'n joio hanes lleol ac yn allweddol yn cychwyn dosbarth hanes lleol y Bynea a Llwynhendy. Roedd hi wedi sôn llawer am ail lyfr hanes, felly diolch yn fawr i'r aelodau ffyddlon am gynhyrchu'r llyfr hwn er cof am Sera.

Sera's square mile was very important to her. She was passionate about local history and instrumental in setting up the Bynea and Llwynhendy local history club. She often spoke about producing another publication, so thank you, faithful members, for producing this book as a lasting memory to Sera.

The 2000 Bynea and Llwynhendy Members

Top Left: Hettie Davies. L/R: Jean Harries, Norah Griffiths, Roger Bateman, Chris Davies, John Saunders, Janet Lloyd, Byron Davies. Front Row: Joey Griffiths, Owena Griffiths (Owners of the Red Cow), Sera Leyshon, Harry Davies, Alun Bowen, Marilyn Bassett. *Photograph by Graham Davies.*

The 2010 Bynea and Llwynhendy Members

L/R: Jean Evans, Merrill Thomas, Merle Davies, Mavis Jenkins, John Smallbones, Joyce Redhorne, John Saunders, Byron Williams, Graham Williams. L/R Front Row: Hettie Davies, Margaret Robinson, Rowland Evans, Anne Llewelyn, Margaret Davies, Chris Davies. Front: Owena Griffiths, Landlady of the "Red Cow". *Photograph by Graham Davies.*

Do you remember?...

Loughor Bridge. *Photograph by Graham Davies.*

Loughor Rail Bridge. *Photograph by Graham Davies.*

Part one
Loughor

Approaching the River Loughor on the A484 you will face the two bridges that spans the river at its narrowest point. These two bridges are a vital link between Glamorgan, Carmarthen, and West Wales

The first road bridge was opened on 24th April 1923, only to be taken down to make way for the second bridge, which was opened in August 1988.

One can still see the original timber that supported the old bridge, in the river bed at low tides.

The railway bridge that runs parallel with the road bridge was opened on Friday September 17th 1852. The original structure was engineered by Brunel, and K. E. Fletcher. It is a Grade 2 listed structure.

Loughor Sands

(Llanelli Star 6th March 2003)

Do you remember the dirt track that led from the road to the railway line?

Below were a series of concrete steps that ran the whole length of the sands, these can still be seen near the railway end. The steps were used by everyone to sit on, and they were able to look down on the stretch of sands which would be very crowded during the summer holidays. As children we played for hours on the sands, and we ate our homemade sandwiches whilst playing. Often our sandwiches would contain more sand than filling but that did not bother us. Then we would walk over the bridge tired but happy to catch the trolley, or the red double decker bus home to Bynea or Llwynhendy.

At the other end of the bridge was the trolley bus terminus. As the trolley reached the works from Llanelli it would turn into the small area and leave by another entrance thus facing back to Llanelli.

Trolley Bus

St. David's Tinplate Works

The St. David's Tinplate works was where my father worked. When the summer was hot they would take the sheets off the side of the works to let some air in. If you were walking on the road you could actually see the men sliding the red hot tinplate to one and other, you could also see the great fly wheel when whistling round at an enormous speed.

I would take bottles of pop to my father when the weather was very hot, they would have a rest and my father would swallow the large bottle of pop in one go. Minutes later the liquid would come out like rain on his body and face.

It was a joy to see the precision of the unit of men handling the hot sheets. The furnace man would slide it along the cast iron floor and my father would fold it over with the tongs, it would then be slid over to the roller man to be squeezed flat and then back into the furnace.

Terry Davies 2010

Workers at St. David's Tinplate Works

(By kind permission of Hettie Davies)

INA Bearings

Yspitty Row, Bynea

INA Bearings

When the old Yspitty Works closed on 1957, a new factory designed to meet the needs of the UK vehicle manufacturing industry was opened on the site where the old tinplate works had stood. INA Bearings was opened in 1966, providing much needed work for the people of the surrounding areas.

Further along, not far from INA Bearings still stands the Lewis Arms public house - a favourite 'watering place' for the tinworkers. Here they would relax after a long day's shift before walking home.

Yspitty Row

Yspitty had a different washing day to the rest of the village. The reason for that being the Steelworks blew out the soot from their big stacks (4 in number) every Monday morning and Yspitty would be snowed with black soot. Occasionally there would be a slight hiccup in the Monday arrangements and the stack would blow out on the Tuesday without informing the Yspitty residents. Then, all the washing would have to be re-washed.

The Bynea Steel Works pond was a great place to fish in. The hot water from the cooling of the mill was ideal to catch gold fish. A stick, some string, a bent pin and a rolled up piece of bread. We would spend hours trying to entice the fish to eat the bread.

Terry Davies 2010

Bynea

After passing Yspitty Row we come to a stretch of road (known to some as 'the Flats'), which leads to the village of Bynea itself, and over the years numerous small light industries have grown up in this area, such as Rees Electrics repairs.

What is the meaning of the name 'Bynea'?, and where did the name originate from. Here are some suggestions that might start you thinking!

Two suggestions for the origins of the name Bynea.

Binea is a Hebrew masculine proper name of uncertain derivation and is thought to mean "fountain". It occurs twice in the Bible as the name of a descendant of Jonathan.

Chronicles 8:37 And Moza begat Binea: Rapha was his son, Eleasah his son, Azel his son:

Chronicles 9:43 And Moza begat Binea; and Rephaiah his son, Eleasah his son, Azel his son.

It seems possible that Bynea Farm was originally owned by a man with this name. Many people had Biblical names in earlier centuries.

Questions have been asked for many decades, "What is the meaning of Bynea?" Could this be the answer?

English – Bynea

Welsh – Binie

Bittern: A marsh bird of genus Botaurus allied to herons; esp. One known for booming note in breeding season.

English; Bittern – plural – Binie.

Welsh; Bittern – singular – Bwn o'r Bannau.

Welsh traditional song "Derin-y-Bwn o'r Bannau."

Bwn (Byniad. Aderyn y bwn. Bwn y gors).

Banllef – Welsh for Booming Sound.

Mel Tonge 2010

Huntsman Corporation

After passing Yspitty we now come to an old familiar building - once the offices of the old Bynea Steel Works. In 1960, the plant was taken over by Texaco. It is now occupied by Huntsman Corporation UK Ltd., which manufactures chemicals.

The electric light illuminates the new steelworks at Bynea, has been given quite a new aspect to the district, it being seen in the evenings for miles around. The two furnaces have already been blasted, while others are in the course of construction. The works have been fitted with all the latest and most up-to-date machinery for the production of steel which, unfortunately will greatly reduce the necessity for manual labour.

Llanelly Mercury Thursday August 11th 1913

Thyssen's Bynea

In 1950s there were a tremendous activity throughout Great Britain to sink new mines as demand for coal exceeded supply. One result was that available shaft sinking firms in the country were overwhelmed, therefore it was decided to ask tenders from abroad, one was received from the German firm Thyssen with whom the contract was finally made.

In 1960, Thyssen transferred the unit into a wholly owned United Kingdom subsidiary company, Thyssen (Great Britain) Ltd., sinking and tunnelling work for the N.C.B. and others throughout Britain. And in those years of expanding to dams for reservoirs, and long tunnels for public water supply, and in due course they set up their headquarters and engineering workshops at Bynea. One notable achievement was constructed during 1970-74 in their workshops at Bynea, a flameproof hard rock tunnel boring machine.

Thyssen (Great Britain) Ltd, found that the centre of gravity of their civil engineering contracts was more in the North of England, so they transferred this company to Yorkshire, bringing to an end their 30 years association with Llanelli.

Extracts of a letter written on the 18/01/2001 to Mr. John Saunders
from Mr. H. A. Hughes, Head of Engineering N.C.B. 1985.

Bwlch Farm

We have now left the 'industrial' side of Bynea, and we have come to where once stood the agricultural part. Here hidden away from the main road lies Bwlch Farm, which once steeped in history, is now a holiday complex.

Bwlch Farm was once a 15th century thatched roofed Longhouse that contained a cowshed and a barn. A stable was also joined to the Longhouse.

When Doctor B.D. and Mrs. E. Hughes moved in, they restored the then dilapidated farm and outhouses into three flats. Later they opened a small agricultural museum from many of their findings that they found on the farm.

The history of the Farm however is very interesting.

Many centuries ago two brothers John & Robert Bonville had built a house on the land of Bwlch Farm with the stones from the estuary. It is thought that a Bonville accompanied William the Conqueror in 1066 when the Normans invaded Britain.

Bynea School

On May 3rd 1897 the new Board School in Bynea opened its doors for the first time, and up to 1976 it had been the 'home' for all the children of Bynea, eager to learn their '3Rs', with the ultimate goal to pass the 11+ and to move on to a flourishing career.

Mr. D.H. Bowen was the first headmaster, and the 178 children were taught by 2 teachers. During the War children were evacuated from London to Bynea and they attended the school; there were 290 children attending the school during those years, however, there was then a decline after the War years.

By 1976 the school had to be closed due to structural damage and it was decided to build a new school further up in the heart of the village off Saron Road.

We all remember the day when we had our group photographs taken in the school yard, or if it was raining in the school hall. Dressed for a school play are some of the early pupils that attended Bynea school.

Also there are a few photographs that range from 1954 to 1968. If you attended Bynea school in those years you may well be in these photographs. Do you recognise yourself and the teachers that taught you ?

Bynea school trip to London 1953.

Bynea School Concert 1936
L/R - Rhoda Evans, Eirwyn Griffiths, Ivor Stroud, Margaret Thomas, Harry Davies, Gweneira Williams, Morwen Thomas, Melville Tonge, Afawny Williams, Gwen Lloyd, Frank Richards.

Llun o blant Ysgol y Bynea ar Ddydd Gŵyl Dewi, Mawrth 1af 1970, gyda eu Prif Athro Mr. Vernon Griffiths.
This photograph of Bynea school children was taken on St. David's Day, March 1st 1970, with them is their Headmaster Mr. Vernon Griffiths.

Care for the community still remains on the ground that cared for so many children for all those years. When the old school was demolished its stones were kept, and the bungalows that were built on the site, now known as 'Tir yr Hên Ysgol', were built from those stones. The old school railings and pillars still remain, as they did for 79 years, to remind the village that 'here stood Bynea School.'

Bynea District Forum

The Forum was initiated in a well attended meeting in the then new Saron Hall in June 1997. The aims were to improve the environment, facilities and quality of life for the residents in the Bynea District. The initial members included county councillor Dillwyn Bowen, councillor Cledwyn Bowen, councillor Marlay Howells, councillor Mairwen Nicholas, Graham Hunt Davies, Terry Davies, Anthony Jones (Businessman), Alison Owen, Kathryn Lewis, Emlyn Rees (Business man), Chris Toft (Works Manager at Huntsman Corporation), Bernard Sheehan, Marion Williams and Gwynne Wooldridge. The officers were elected by the committee and consisted of Gwynne Wooldridge (chairman), Kathryn Lewis (secretary) and Graham Hunt Davies (treasurer).

A Forum map was agreed stretching from Loughor Bridge in the East, Penygraig in the North, Erw Las in the west and the foreshore in the South. The constitution was formulated with the election of members every three years. Committee meetings were held every month with an Annual General Meeting every June.

In 1997, a detailed questionnaire was distributed including some sixty questions asking residents, in the Forum Area, to outline their wishes and concerns. Three quarters of the questionnaires were filled in and returned, with the outcomes analysed in detail by the Department of European Studies in Swansea University College.

The main concerns expressed by these returns showed a strong desire by the residents for an improvement in the environment and facilities in the Forum area

The early years involved the Forum opposing detrimental industrial developments such as the Asphalt Plant in the centre of the village, a Coal fired Power Station at Berwick, a Traveller site in the village confines and the establishment of a Recycling Facility in the former Taybrite Works. It was clearly understandable that local residents, particularly those in Yspitty near Loughor Bridge, had suffered enough over the years from the unfriendly polluting type industries.

In 2000, a breakthrough came in the restoration of the 200 year old Genwen Quarry Engine House following grants from CADW and Carmarthenshire County Council. This was followed by a detailed Feasibility Study of the 15 acre Genwen Quarry by Wardell Armstrong Consultants, with a view of turning the quarry into a picturesque community and wildlife park. This is still ongoing and will be the eventual jewel in the crown of the Forum's achievements.

Working very closely with Family Housing and Carmarthenshire County Council, 'Tir Yr Hen Ysgol 'bungalows for the elderly was opened on the site of the old Bynea Primary School in 2001. The old stone and yellow bricks of the old school were incorporated into the innovative 'Portmeirion' design.'

The new Bynea Square was opened on Saint David's Day 2008, with a detailed village interpretive board at the centre of the Celtic cross and stonework design. The local Bynea Primary School children had contributed significantly to the history board. The Swirl Cone artwork on our Eastern Entrance off Loughor Bridge was completed in June 2008 to much acclaim and some controversy.

The latest large project has been the installation of the original Stradey Park iconic goalposts on the Berwick roundabout in 2009 near the new Parc y Scarlets.

To date, the incorporation of the old Engine Fach orchard into the cartilage of Bynea Primary School with a gateway, bridge and fencing has been the icing on the cake of the very significant achievements of the dedicated members of Bynea District Forum over the last 13 years, which have brought in significant funding to benefit this much loved and very special area called Bynea.

E. R. Edwards & Sons
(Evan Rees Edwards)
1893 -1974

E.R. Edwards & Son (Edward Rees Edwards) started his business in Bynea 'Ivy House' Cwmfelin Road, in approximately 1893. He traded in this property as a general grocers for 15 years. In 1908 he decided to build a larger premises, this being situated on land opposite Bynea Station. The shop was known as 'Supply Stores' and was built by R. M. Griffiths of Llwynhendy at the cost of £363. It took 9 months to build and they moved in on the 11th March 1908.

The 'Supply Stores' in every sense of the word sold a variety of products. Groceries - general food items, with their own blend of tea. Evan Rees was the first to introduce tinned fruit to the area, and opened the tin in the shop, as tin openers were not readily available at the time.

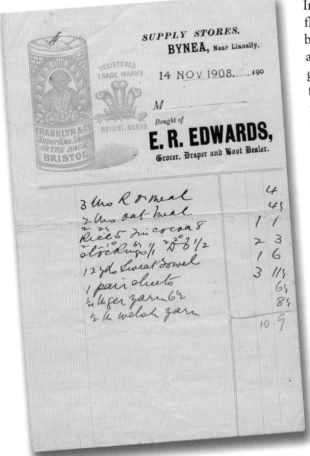

In the drapery department he sold flannel shirts for men in the steel works, blouses, skirts, lace aprons for girls and women in domestic service, caps, gloves, overcoats and suites to order. In the Haberdashery Department he sold material by the yard, cotton thread, ribbons, elastic, and all sewing needs, also large ornate hat pins.

Tin Baths, pots and pans brushes and rugs were also sold. Grain for the poultry was delivered to Bynea station every month solely for E.R. Edwards.

In 1924 it was decided to build an extension to the shop, the builder being Eddie William Davies of Loughor. Now he introduced newspapers, sweets and cigarettes, and Christmas time he sold

This invoice shows a reference to the Tin works in Bynea, i.e. '12 yards of sweat towel' which would have been used by the employees.

elaborate range of boxed chocolates, and during the summer time fresh ice cream was made daily at the shop which was very popular with those playing tennis in the tennis court behind the shop.

Bess the horse who pulled the cart delivered goods around the district. She hated going over the old Loughor bridge, which was wooden and often bolted across at high speed, almost losing the load in the river below. They delivered goods to a very large area Loughor, Three Crosses, and Fforestfach.

Graham, Jestyn, and Maelgwyn were the three sons, who continued running the business until it finished in 1974.

Maelgwyn had to turn the handle of the ice cream machine for hours, something he had to do, being the youngest!

Anna Edwards 2010

Nº 00198

Memo from

E. R. EDWARDS & SONS

H. G. EDWARDS, C. J. EDWARDS, I. M. EDWARDS

SUPPLY STORES, BYNEA
LLANELLI

Telephone : 3949 Llanelli

VAT No. 122 2839 91
Reg. Swansea

Our Ref.............. *Shop*   Your Ref......................

M.............. *Finished Trading 1974*

.............................19.........................

216
STRAND,
W·C

Twinings

TEAMEN·TO
H·M·THE·KING

H·R·H·THE
PRINCE·OF·WALES

CHRISTMAS·AND
NEW·YEAR·GIFTS

CASWELL & BOWDEN'S COALS

BROWN & POLSON'S

CORN FLOUR

BOVRIL

"A HAPPY THOUGHT"

Bringing Home Warmth & Health

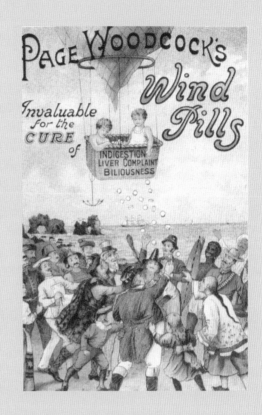

Here are some advertisements that were around in the early years of business, and some are even around today. How Many can you recognise?

Old Bynea Bridge

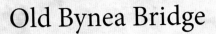

The following poem was acclaimed the 'Best Verse' at the Eisteddfod held in Bynea on Saturday 16th November 1941. It was written by Master David Temple a evacuee residing in Bynea. (reported in the Llanelly Mercury Thursday 21st November 1941).

The Old Bynea Bridge
Old Bynea bridge is small but strong
Along it pass a merry throng
Of people to their work each day
And those who while their time away.

Beneath it runs the railway line
A station too, I think it's fine
There also is a signal box
And as the trains rush by it rocks.

Thus after writing this I say
That if they ever come this way
Go, visit this fair bridge of old
It is a pleasure to behold.

Bynea Road, now known as Cwmfelin Road. To the right is the old Post Office
and the entrance to the Plâs, now Brynhelyg Residential Home.

David Harry - The Squire of Bynea

In the late 1950's I was asked to empty the contents and dispose of them by burning books and records of the old family. There were book records of David Harry's Business Transactions relating to the early1900's onwards, and I was amazed at the extent of his land holdings (farms etc) and had large holdings in most of the coal mines in the area. The books were beautifully registered in copper plate handwriting. He had a Mining Engineering Degree.

There would be share holdings in the Llanelli Light as well as shares world wide. New Zealand Railway Company, and the Australian Railways Company, and all major companies you could think of. He was a truly an astonishing entrepreneur. The black chauffeur driven car would glide out of the Plâs (Palace) with David Harry sitting in the back, a hunched up little figure muffled and blanketed. As children we would play football with a small ball and the car would stop, the window would wind down and he would say, "that is the wrong shaped ball you are playing with" in a gruff voice.

A very influential benefactor to Soar Chapel. He donated the strip of land opposite Soar, (now fenced in) opposite the Soar gates. There he built stone pillars, a gate, and a seat where he could sit on to view all his farmland holdings, down to the estuary.

Terry Davies 2010

Joey and Owena Griffiths

When the Bynea and Llwynhendy History Society was formed in 1997 it was immediately accepted that its natural home would be at the Red Cow public house. The Society continues to meet there on a regular basis up to the present time, and its continued connection with the establishment is owed in no small measure to the genial landlady, Owena Griffiths.

Owena, and her late and fondly remembered husband, Joey, took over the place when Joey's mother, the matriarch of the family, Anita, retired from the trade in 1983 at the age of 84, after reigning supreme behind the bar for 53 years. Joey and Owena were splendid hosts and provided comforts and facilities conducive to a friendly, happy atmosphere at the Society's monthly meetings.

Joey did not enjoy good health in his later years but did sometimes contribute to the meetings regaling us with anecdotes about his days growing up in a pub ambience. One such is Joey recalling, facetiously perhaps, the days long before passive smoking was considered a health hazard when men engaged in the local heavy industries of the area would call for a pint after the end of their shift. The atmosphere was dense with tobacco smoke, so much so, Joey said, that at times one could detect in the air three different layers of tobacco smoke, depending on the quality and strength of the tobacco used. Indeed, Joey attributed his latent ill health to his exposure at a young age to such an atmosphere. Of great interest to the group was the Griffiths family's artefacts and documents relating back to the early years of the establishment, and it is gratifying to know that these are in Owena and her family's safe keeping. Another member of the family who put in an appearance occasionally was the lovable George, a Great Dane, whose docility belled his appearance. He would sometimes pop his head over the bar counter, cast an eye over the clientele, and return quietly to his quarters satisfied that everything was in order.

After Joey's death, Owena has more or less managed the business single handedly, maintaining the traditional high standards of the house, and in these days of accelerating pub closures it is pleasing to note that the Red Cow still retains the status of a 'local' The Society could not wish for a more amiable, thoughtful host who has served us well, and continues to do so. It has been my pleasant duty to record this tribute to Joey and Owena for their excellent service over the years.

Byron Davies, May 2010.

Please to give him 2^d worth of beer and give him 1 pint
Mrs Phillips

please to give 2 shillings
worth of beer to me
if you please
because i cant come
up myself tonight

Red Cow and Cwmfelin Row

Côr Meibion Cwmfelin

Formed in the tiny village of Bynea near Llanelli in 1964, Côr Meibion Cwmfelin has grown from the initial handful of singers to its present membership of 120 voices. Rehearsals were held in Bynea School but have now moved to larger school at Llwynhendy. Most of the members work at British Steel Corporation's Trostre works. They began competitive singing last year coming second at Cardigan and third at Porthcawl Miners Eisteddfod. Denver Philips,B.A., conductor and Eifion Thomas, accompanist, who have both been with the choir since its inception, led them at their first National this year. Registered as a Chief Male Choir, it has given over 40 concerts for charity, rapidly gaining in experience and reputation.

They later became known as Côr Meibion Llanelli.

The Butchers Arms, Bynea

A young, ambitious couple came to Bynea village in 1851 residing in 9 Cwmfelin Row where baby Hannah (my grandmother) the first of 10 children was born. Shortly afterwards 1861 census states that Titus and Margaret were 'Grocers'. This must have been a successful business because a little later on they were recorded as being 'Grocers and Publicans' of 'The Butchers Arms'(called 'The Bwt' for short). Appropriately named as this enterprising couple took advantage of the necessity in the village for fresh meat and all household requirements to be conveniently to hand. According to my father, who from a very young age helped in the grocery business of his mother Hannah at Pantyglien, and his grandparents at the two shops called 'Peoples Stores' and 'Supply Stores', Cwmfelin, where it is reported in Llanelly Mercury August 1913 she died. His grand-parents, instigated by his grandmother Margaret, started a smallholding by keeping two sheep and a few pigs and undoubtedly chickens in the field behind, which entitled him to be recorded in a later census as 'A farmer' while his daughter Elizabeth and her husband John Ungoed ran the Public House and Shop. In that era one could slaughter ones own livestock and this Titus did, selling joints around the houses. (No Health and Safety restrictions).

According to the census he had plenty of scope to develop with 30 acres of land, thus supplying villagers with food, household requirements, meat and alcoholic refreshments, being once fined for selling alcohol after hours. (No twenty-four hour drinking.)

By 1867 baby Hannah was also growing up to be a Shopkeeper and 1872 had two shops trading.

October 23rd 1880 my father was born in 'The Butchers'. My mother told me the story that there was a Fair in the locality and the servant Anne Roberts, age 17 was allowed time off. My father arrived while she was away. Returning she remarked "Oedd rhaid i'r diawl bach dod heno".

Titus retired and lived in one of the two houses attached to 'The Butchers' while Elizabeth, his daughter and her husband John Ungoed, carried on with the public house at the same time they had a large family of 13 children.

On the 1st July 1915 a lease was taken out between Elizabeth Ungoed and others. To Buckleys Brewery for 21 years at a rental of £60.00 per annum. This was covering the public house, garden and stables at the rear. It was then insured for £500. This makes very interesting reading but too long to publish here.

John and Elizabeth retired near to some of their children who went down New Dock area to keep Public houses and grocery businesses, while others went into professions. Buckleys Brewery employed stewards to run the pub, while younger generations lived in the two houses attached. Villagers recall one nephew residing in the end house nick-named 'Titws' (I am told means 'little Titus').

The shop was by this time run by the "Gunn" family.

In 1966 it was sold to Bynea Rugby Club. This was a fitting transaction as nostalgically the original board is now on the wall of the Club with Titus Jones as the 2nd Captain in 1884-1885 and his grandson Frederick Glyn, known as Harry Ungoed was playing for the team 1920-1921 and was on the committee who started the Club in 1919 according to the centenary book and became Captain of the London Welsh. Also recorded in the Rugby Centenary Book is that son of the Butchers Arms is reputed to have bought the first Rugby Ball in the village, which was even then the Headquarters of the Club, a local headmaster. While generations onward my twin grandsons Nicholas and Christian Davies played for the Bynea Rugby Club in 2001. Nicholas returned to Bynea Rugby Football Club as a player and Coach in 2009 and remains with the Club.

The upper floor, where the family used to meet every Sunday,(no work was allowed to be done), from all parts of the surrounding areas, My cousin., Della Davies, Bynea who remembers her grandmother Elizabeth very well told me that this is where all the family business was discussed and arranged, to the extent that when Hannah's daughter Mary was left a widow with a six week old baby and her uncle David Hopkins left a young widower with two young boys, the family decided that they should marry, and this they did, raising three other children and living in Parc Eynon Farm, now demolished to make way for the Wildlife Centre.

Whilst delivering groceries to his eldest sister in Gorseinon from his mother's shop my father met my mother, it was not possible for a love match to take place then, as she, being only five years old living in Trinity Road, Gorseinon went to call his niece Beatrice out to play. My father answered the door and when my mother asked in Welsh "Gall Beatrice dod allan i chwarae" that was their first meeting He was then fifteen years old.. Incidentally, they did not marry until many years later and spoke only Welsh to each other throughout their married lives, living until 91 years and 92 years old respectively.

The upper floor of the Butchers Arms has been an Indian Restaurant in recent years and I wonder what would be the reaction of the old people if they stood outside and looked up at it, but they must surely be looking down remembering how successful they were in the village of Bynea enabling them to not only provide and educate their 10 children but also be there for their grandchildren and great-grandchildren of whom my generation are deservedly proud.

Margaret Hannah Davies, 2010.

A special tea party was arranged by the Taberbacle and Saron Sunday Schools for the children to celebrate 25 years ministry of the Rev. David Hopkins. Children presented him with a clock - they succeeded in making the collection secretly.

Llanelly Mercury Thursday October 2nd 1941

The History of Saron Community Hall

The origins of the current Saron Community Hall in Bynea goes back to 1887 when Tabernacle Chapel Llwynhendy rented the Bynea Board School in order to hold a Sunday school. This eventually resulted in the Chapel purchasing a plot of land known as `Y Rhedyn Bach` from Mrs Lucy Lewis, Pencoed and her daughter Mrs Mary Jane Jones, Isgoed.

The work started in 1903, and the building was completed in January 1904. Costing Tabernacle members £417 10s. 9d, Saron was officially opened on the 5th & 6th of February 1904 A second piece of land was then purchased from Jacob Jenkins allowing Saron to have an entrance from the main road.

Since then Saron has been the host for many societies in the area - annual Eisteddfods; meeting place for choirs; committee meetings, and parties. The Bynea Urdd was started in Saron in 1924. It was used by Berea Chapel in 1934 and Zion Apostolic Church when Zion roof required replacing in the late 1960s.

As the years went by it was no longer feasible to keep the building open so it was sold to Llanelli Rural Council, and with financial assistance from the European Union, Saron opened once again as the Saron Community Hall in 1996. Saron is once more the thriving place for the people of Bynea, as it was when it first opened its doors in 1904.

Extracts from the notes of the late Sera Leyshon, on `Saron Community Hall` By kind permission of her mother Beth Leyshon.

The New Bynea Primary School

The new Bynea Primary School, situated in Saron Road, Bynea, was officially opened on 20th February, 1976.

Then, with an increasing number of pupils on roll, an additional extension was built onto the existing school building and was officially opened on 13th November, 2003.

Currently, there are 97 pupils on roll and from April 2010 the school was granted Nursery Provision for 3 year olds. Mrs Tania Morgan, current Headteacher of Ysgol y Bynea has been in post since April 2009.

Part Two
Bynea Station

Having reached the end of our journey through the main street of Bynea we have to retrace our steps back to Bynea Station. Coming down the steps we face Station Road, and our journey begins.

According to the Llanelly Guardian in April 1901 the new Great Western Railway station was completed at Bynea. Replacing the dilapidated shanty which had done the duty for so many years. There were waiting rooms on both sides, and there was also a handsome bridge. The station also acquired a booking office but only on the up platform. Bynea station now is just two bare platforms – a halt on the 'Heart of Wales' line.

Bynea Railway Station.

Station Road - to the left of this photograph stood the four cottages mentioned in the Glossop tales.

Glossop's Gentleman of the Road

We knew it was spring when the Glossop man came with his home on iron wheels with a little chimney on the roof. He was the Tar Man laying new roads and paths for the council. He was a larger than life character with a magnificent handle bar moustache that protruded a good 3 inches each side of his face. Now he lived permanently in this little shed on wheels, and in the evening he would light his fire and then he would sit on the back smoking a large pipe, all the children were fascinated by him.

Every night he would go to Maggie's chip shop for his supper (either fish or rissole and chips) and when he had finished eating, he would rub the grease from the chip paper and would wax his moustache with it, twirling the ends into points. He would then rub the chip paper on his hair, so that it was well greased. He always parked close to the Plough Inn where the old cottages stood in line with the bridge wall. These cottages were called 1, 2, 3, & 4 Dyffryn Arel.

Terry Davies 2010

The Gospel Hall

The Gospel Hall has stood on this site since 1926 and retains a warmth of welcome for any visitors. Numbers have now declined but the tradition of working with children has continued.

Rowland Evans 2010

The Ghost of Pencoed Colliery Lamp Room

The old Colliery pond is still at Pencoed Farm, the old site of the Pencoed Colliery. In the early part of the last century a 17 year old girl fell pregnant. The boy would not marry her and she could not live with the stigma and shame, so one evening she committed suicide by drowning in the pond.

The only structure left of the old colliery is the little lamp room which has seen many uses. There has been many reports of sightings of this young girl's presence, none more so than when it became a Pentecostal Church for a period of time, no doubt attracted by the very loud singing on a Sunday, which could be heard in Penderi. The farm owner has closed the building for many years, and Margaret Jones tells me should would not enter that building to save her life.

Terry Davies 2010

The remains of the old lead works at Pencoed.

Photograph of the Bynea and Llwynhendy History Group on their ramble to 'y pownd Pencoed' - the pond Pencoed.

Memorial Pillar

The Memorial Pillar on the little railway bridge in Penderi, which ran from Pencoed Colliey down the incline (passing Terry Davies' house).

The Inscription on the bridge reads as follows:-

DYFFRYN DISASTER TRAIN
OCTOBER 1904

GENWEN PIT EXPLOSION
MARCH 1907

GLYNEA PIT EXPLOSION
OCTOBER 1913 & 1919

TITANIC SUNK 1912

WALLY

Demolition of Penderi Bridge with neighbours gathering to witness the event.

Genwen Colliery Beam and Parallel Pumping Engine

This engine was installed at the Genwen Colliery at around the same time as Chaucer Townsend's Canal. The problem of flooding at the lower seams was acute as the 80 metre fiery vein was a much thicker seam than the 40 yards Swansea Vein. So, it was far more profitable to mine the lower seam.

The installation of the Cornish Beam Engine made it possible to locate the recovery of the coal, but having increased the production they saturated the surrounding area and as there were no means of transporting the coal. Chauncer Townsend came up with the brilliant idea of selling it further afield. Consequently it became necessary to build a provision for the purpose. The Genwen Canal came into being to enable the coal to be exported to foreign lands, France Portugal, Ireland and Cornwall where quality rich coal was in high demand.

The canal would run from the Genwen to the Glynea Colliery and then down to the Estuary approximately a mile long. It was dug out by hand 26 feet wide by 6ft deep. It was a two year contract, and the job was undertaken by twelve men. The contract price being

£59.00 which was a considerable sum in those days. The canal was finished in 18 months and it was used for the next 15 years until the advent of Railways came into being.

One interesting note when Chauncer Townsend built the Bynea Canal was that he had plans to extend the system. He had approached Lord Cawder to extend the canal to Llandeilo, but Lord Cawdor refused him permission to cross his land. I would assume the canal would have transported wood which was plentiful there.

Terry Davies 2010

LLANELLY MERCURY, THURSDAY, MARCH 7. 1907.

PIT BLAST AT LLWYN-HENDY.

RESCUERS BAFFLED BY THE AFTER-DAMP.

SIX MINERS LOST.

TWO RESCUERS PERISH.

A very sad explosion took place at the Genwen Colliery, Llwynhendy, on Tuesday evening, and when the news was circulated that four miners were down in the pit, and could not be found, the whole district was plunged into intense grief. The names of the unfortunate persons were Tom Davies, Heol, Llwynhendy; David Phillips, Stradey House, Llwynhendy; Thomas Howells, Penygraig, Llwynhendy, and Llewellyn Evans, Penderry, Llwynhendy.

It was fortunate that at the time the explosion occurred the number of men at the colliery was comparatively small. Strenuous efforts had already been made to reach the men, but the rescuing party were baffled by the afterdamp, and could make no headway into the workings. Two of them, named Roderick Davies, of Llangennech, and Edward Harry, near Yspytty, Bynea, had not returned by mid-day on Wednesday, and their fate, together with the four unfortunate miners, was unknown.

News of the explosion spread very rapidly through the village, and, naturally, great anxiety was felt for the safety of the men underground. People flocked to the pit's mouth, and waited with bated breath for any news which would give some indication as to whether the men were likely to be rescued alive. The scene when it was announced that the rescuing party had been driven back by the afterdamp, and that two had been overcome, was touching to a degree, but notwithstanding the keen disappointment, it was still hoped that the worst had not befallen the unfortunate men, and that subsequent efforts to reach them would prove more successful. The colliery, which is by no means a small one, is owned by Messrs. Harry Bros.

P.S. Samuel Jones, Llanelly, was soon in attendance, and, together with P.C. Tom Davies and P.C. Jenkins, and a number of workmen, did everything possible to satisfy the anxiety of the crowd on the surface.

Mr. Beynon, the under-manager, and Mr. D. Meredith, together with Messrs. Harry Bros., worked most energetically, and were down in the pit with the rescuers for several hours, Messrs. Joseph Harry and Daniel Meredith being down all through Tuesday night.

When our reporter again visited the place on Wednesday morning it was learnt that the efforts to rescue the men over-night had been unavailing.

Rescue parties were organised, and a large number came forward to offer their help. The first rescue party consisted of Messrs. Joseph Harry, Llew. Jones, Robert Phillpot, and Evan Winter, but these had to return in consequence of the after-damp. Subsequently, another party went down, comprising Messrs. Daniel Williams, James Nicholas, Samuel Davies, Dd. Samuel, David Bowen, Jos. Harries, and D. Jenkins. Their efforts again proved futile, and so overcome were they by the after-damp that they had to be attended to by doctors. Many of them were unconscious, and were only just saved.

Several ladies also offered their assistance, and provided refreshments for the rescuers. Mrs. Jenkins, Mrs. Edwards, and Mrs. Harry supplied coffee, and Miss Davies, schoolmistress, supplied milk. Their generosity in this direction was greatly valued.

The mine is known to be gassy, and the gravest fears were entertained for the unfortunate men's safety. Had the explosion occurred a little earlier, the result must have been terrible, for a number of workmen had only just left the workings when it took place. The four men would have come up at the same time, if it had not been that they had to clear some headings.

SCENE AT THE COLLIERY.

The scene at the mouth of the pit was a sorry one, and manifestations of sincere regret were expressed on all hands. There was a large crowd of men and women who had been in weary vigil for any intelligence, and wherever one went, the question was, "Any news?" Mr. J. Dyer Lewis, H.M. Inspector of Mines for the Swansea District, was soon in attendance, and he, in company with Messrs. John Knoyle, J. E. Burnell, Joseph Harry, Arthur John, and Albert Harding, formed another rescue party. They went down to the pit about 11.30 in the morning, and everyone hoped that the mission would be more successful, and that they would not share the fate of the two would-be rescuers that had previously gone down, and were still in the pit.

INTERVIEW WITH MR. DAVID HARRY.

In an interview Mr. David Harry explained that the explosion took place about 6.30 p.m. on Tuesday, when there were only four men underground. He spoke with great emotion, and added that an explosion of gas had taken place on the face.

"When we went down, the gas came full in our faces. At the time the explosion occurred we did not hear anything but the engine-man on the bank saw smoke coming up. We went for Mr. Beynon, the under-manager, who went down the pit. Subsequently, my brother and I went down, and found that the stoppings were a bit shaken. Our endeavours to put them in order proved very successful, and we were also very successful in getting fairly close to the men."

"Was there any after-damp then?"

"It was terrible, and we had to fight hard against it. No doubt, the after-damp was due to the fact that these stoppings were leaking. Oh! yes, we were very successful in carrying on the work, and there was plenty of volunteers to go down the pit. In fact, we had one trouble in stopping them. Daniel Meredith was foremost among the rescuers, and he and my brother Joseph were down all night. By no means down until 2 o'clock, and I advised him to go to rest with the others."

"Have you had any trouble with the gas before, Mr. Harry?"

"No; we have enjoyed complete immunity from any trouble by gas. We must say that we are very grateful for the abundant help offered."

Referring to the unfortunate men down in the pit, Mr. Harry stated: "We never had better men. They were most trustworthy and honourable, and each bore a fine moral character."

MR. DAVID HARRY OVERCOME.

During yesterday afternoon a sad turn took place to the rescue work, Mr. David Harry being carried out of the colliery, suffering from the effects of the after-damp. Mr. Harry, as already stated, was down in the pit all through Tuesday night and some parts of yesterday, and so weak had he become that he could not stand the strain, and was overcome. He was conveyed to a neighbouring house, where a doctor attended him.

ANOTHER SAD INCIDENT.

Another pathetic incident in connection with the occurrence is that the son of Thomas Howells, one of the entombed miners, died on Tuesday, and his wife is in a very collapsed state, having had to take to her bed.

VERY LITTLE HOPE.

When our reporter paid another visit to the spot, about 7.30 last night, the unfortunate men had not been found, and the anxiety of the crowd was much more intense. Still, the work of endeavouring to rescue went on, but there was apparently little hope of the men being brought up alive. The operations of the rescue party were very slow, owing to the effect of the after-damp.

GENWEN EXPLOSION

SMOKING PIPES FOUND, AND TWO LAMPS OPEN.

OPENING OF THE INQUEST.

FUNERALS OF THE VICTIMS.

The pessimistic impression that all the six men who were down in the Genwen Colliery, Cwmfelin, had perished proved only too true. Although things looked very black, there was hope after all that some of the unfortunate colliers at the pit might be rescued alive, but the hope was ruthlessly shattered.

In the first hour of Thursday, the bodies of the two would-be rescuers, Edward Harry and Roderick Davies, were discovered in the heading, about 30 yards from the deep, by Oliver Meredith, Daniel Meredith, and David John Harry, the last-named a brother of Edward Harry.

Then about 7 a.m. on Thursday, the bodies of Llewellyn Evans and Thomas Howells were recovered, and those of David Phillips and Thomas Davies about 9.30.

It will be remembered that Edward Harry and Roderick Davies, eager to render assistance to the entombed men, were amongst the rescuing party who first descended the pit. Instead of going towards the in-take airway, they rushed towards the outlet way, and in the absence of fresh air were overcome by the foul gas.

All the bodies were carried to the blacksmith's shop close to the colliery.

The two rescuers were the only unmarried men among the victims. Both were trammers at the colliery, and were about 20 years of age. Llewellyn Evans' watch was found in the pit, and had stopped at 3.25. The explosion could not have taken place at that time, and the probability is that he had forgotten to wind it the night before.

FOUR WIDOWS; TWELVE ORPHANS.

As already reported, the six victims are—
Llewellyn Evans, Penddery; married; four children.

Thomas Howells, Llwynhendy; married; two children.

David Phillips, Llwynhendy; married; six children.

Thomas Davies, Tyrmynydd, married; two children.

Edward Harry, Yspitty; single.

Roderick Davies, Llangennech; single.

Mr. Arthur Williams, son of Mr. Dan Williams, J.P., was in charge of the gang which discovered the bodies of Llewllyn Evans and Thomas Howells. Among those who assisted were Mr. William Clement, under-manager at Pencoed Colliery; Mr. John Beynon, under-manager of the Genwen Colliery; Mr. David Phillips and Mr. William Evans. The food boxes of the two men were empty.

BROTHER FINDS BROTHER.

David John Harry found the body of his brother, Edward Harry, and subsequently the body of Roderick Davies, about thirty yards from the bottom of the slant.

In an interview Harry said that his brother ran wildly down the pit.

"Yes, he thought I was working down below. In his excitement, he went down the wrong way."

"Were you expected to be down there at six o'clock?"

"I would have been working at the colliery at the time had I not been detained an hour or so in the morning. My brother did not know of this, and he fully believed that I was down in the pit."

"What time did you arrive on the scene?"

"I was to start at six o'clock. I was about going down when the engine-man discovered the smoke issuing from the shaft. Another minute and I would have been down, and would of course have met with the same fate as these poor fellows."

AN UNFOUNDED REPORT.

The report that the son of Thomas Howells, one of the victims, was dead is incorrect. The child is very poorly, but as yet alive. His widow, and Evans' widow, are both in very poor health.

A STARTLING DISCOVERY.

It was authoritatively ascertained that the searching party had made certain discoveries, which are sufficient to explain the cause of the disaster.

When the dead bodies were recovered on Thursday, it was found that three pipes, filled with tobacco, had been used. Two were wooden pipes, the third being an ordinary clay pipe. The pipes had been half-smoked, and to all appearances pointed to the fact that a whiff was being enjoyed when death came upon them with all its horrors. It is stated that one of the victims actually had his pipe in his hand.

Another and an equally sinister discovery was the finding of two lamps unlocked. The colliery is one worked with locked lamps, and the significance of two lamps being found open will be at once realized.

A PATHETIC INCIDENT.

One of the most pathetic sights in the tragedy was to see young Willie Phillips, the eldest son of David Phillips, spending the whole of his time from Tuesday night until Wednesday night in weary vigil at the pit's mouth, and patiently watching and refusing to leave without his father.

THE INQUEST.

EVIDENCE OF IDENTIFICATION.

David Rees Davies, Dimpath, Llanelly, stated that he saw the bodies at the colliery, and the one nearest to the door of the blacksmith's shop was that of his brother, Thomas Davies, who lived at Llwynhendy. Deceased was a collier employed at the Genwen Colliery, which belonged to Messrs. Harry Brothers. Deceased was 45 years of age.

John Phillips, Brynhaul, Llwynhendy, deposed that the body which was second from the door at the colliery was that of his brother, David Phillips. Deceased was 42 years of age.

Joseph Harry, Lletrog, Bryn, deposed that the third body from the doorway was that of his brother-in-law, named Thomas Howells, who lived at Penygraig, and worked at the Genwen Colliery as a collier. Deceased was 26 years of age.

John Beynon, Caegwyn, Cwmfelin, deposed that he was the under-manager at Genwen Colliery. The fourth body from the doorway was that of Llewelyn Evans, Maesyffynon, who was a collier. Deceased was his brother-in-law, and was 38 years of age.

David John Harry, Cwmfelin Row, identified the body of Edward Harry as his brother. Deceased resided at Pantyglien, and was employed as a trammer at Genwen Colliery. Deceased was 20 years of age.

William Davies, Maes Road, Llangennech, deposed that the last body as the jury entered the blacksmiths' shop at the colliery was that of Roderick Davies, who was his brother. Deceased was engaged as a trammer at Genwen Colliery, and was 19 years of age.

MEDICAL TESTIMONY.

Dr. J. L. Davies, Llanelly, deposed that he saw the bodies of Thomas Davies, David Phillips, Llewelyn Evans, and Thomas Howells that morning. He examined them and found that death was due to inhalation of carbon-monoxide gas. There were very serious and severe burns of the chest, arms, and the whole of the head. With one exception there were no other external injury.

The Coroner: Were they all extensively burnt?—Yes, every part upon which there was no clothing.

Llewelyn Evans had the fractured leg?—Yes, and he had a fracture of small bones near the ankle.

Did these men live long, do you think?—No, and death must have been almost instantaneous in each case.

Did you also examine the bodies of Edward Harry and Roderick Davies?—Yes.

What do you attribute the cause of death to?—Syncope. They were asphyxiated.

How long do you think these men lived after they were overcome?—Very few minutes.

Witness added: "I might say that the attitude of the arms in each case was as if protecting their faces.

The Coroner: That was how you saw them?

Witness: Yes.

The inquiry was then adjourned until March 22nd.

FUNERALS OF THE VICTIMS.

The village of Llwynhendy wore a gloomy aspect on Saturday, when the unfortunate miners were interred amidst every manifestation of public mourning and sympathy.

Owing to the fact that the body of David Phillips, Stradey, Llwynhendy, had to be interred at the graveyard connected with Tabernacle Baptist Chapel, this funeral started 2.30. The house of the deceased is close to the burial ground, and a crowd of mourners lined the route. A short service having been conducted by the Rev. B. Williams (pastor) of the chapel, assisted by the Rev. H. Jones, Bethel, Llanelly, the "Dead March," from "Saul," was impressively played as the mourners left.

The funerals of Thomas Davies, Thomas Howells, Llewellyn Evans, and Edward Harry were timed to start at 3.30, and the cortege met at Soar Baptist Chapel simultaneously, the coffins being borne on biers. Spacious as Soar Chapel is, it proved far too small to accommodate the hundreds of persons anxious to attend the memorial service. The "Dead March" was played as the four coffins were reverently carried along the aisle, and the congregation then impressively sang "Cofia f'enaid cyn it' dreulio." The Rev. J. Lewis, Calsalem, Llanelly, having read a portion of Scripture, touching references were made to the catastrophe by the Rev. B. Williams (Tabernacle), Rev. J. Evans (Bryn), Rev. Trevor Jones (Bethania), Rev. Hugh Jones (Bethel), and the Rev. J. R. Davies (Soar), "Bydd myrdd o ryfeddodau" was then sung and the bodies were interred in the adjoining cemetery in the following order:—Llewellyn Evans, Thomas Howells, Thomas Davies, and Edward Harry.

The body of Roderick Davies, one of the two young rescuers, was buried at Bethesda Chapel, Llangennech, amidst deep sorrow. The Rev. D. Davies (pastor) and the Rev. Mr. Morris impressively officiated. The attendance was a very large one.

MABON'S PROTEST.

HIS PLEA FOR THE GENWEN VICTIMS

The monthly meeting of the Rhondda District of Miners was held at Porth on Monday, Mr. T. I. Jones, Ferndale, presiding.

Mr. W. Abraham (Mabon), M.P., called attention to what he characterised as the villifying of the victims of the Genwen Pit, Llanelly, in the press. He did not think that he was exaggerating when he said that his heart bled on seeing the headings of a paragraph in one of the evening papers on Saturday. There in bold type they had such headings as "Inviting Death" and "Six Lives for a Smoke." With all the energy that he possessed he protested against the villifying of these unfortunate men, who had paid with their lives the penalty for any fault that they might have committed. This sort of thing gave the impression to the man in the street that there was no blame attached to anybody except the workman, but they who knew something about colliery work would realise the fact that the workings must have been a kind of "living gasometer" before men where taking their food, even though they had a thousand pipes. He did not for a moment excuse men for any fault that they might have committed, but he took exception to a verdict being passed upon them before a proper inquiry was made. But what about the two men who had lost their lives in seeking for their comrades? Where was the discipline of the colliery to allow young men to rush excitedly down the pit into the afterdamp, for the fact that they missed their way in such a small colliery proved that they were not in a fit state to have undertaken the task? And that he pleaded was that the memories of these men should not be further villified.

Flower and Vegetable Show

Once every year the Hall would be decked out for the long awaited show. Now there was huge competition for the coveted Gold Award. Nearly everyone in the village had a garden and the size of some produce was a joy to see, the best leeks, heavy weight pumpkins, giant potatoes, runner beans as long as your arm and apples of every description.

The competition was fierce with secret formulas for the best produce. The most popular myth of secret formula being Sunday morning urine after drinking copious amounts of beer on Saturday night!

BYNEA SHOW

The Bynea annual horticultural show, ambulance and rifle shooting competitions on Saturday last proved a great success in every respect. There was a record number of entries in the horticultural section, and the exhibits were of a high standard. Keen interest was shown in the ambulance competition, and the rifle shooting competition also proved a great attraction. The president was Mr. John Thomas, Bwlch, and the vice-president was Mr. David Eynon, Ffosfach. Chairman of committee and chief steward, Mr. W. R. Rolfe; treasurer, Mr. Aneurin Davies; joint secretaries, Messrs. Jonah Morris and Joseph Davies. Judges: Horticulture, Mr. R. Davies, Llanfynydd Road, Carmarthen; Welsh cakes and preserved fruit, Mrs. Henry Richards, Trallwm Road, Llwynhendy. For the most number of points, Mr. Jabez Thomas, Gwynfryn, was the winner of the silver cakestand, which was presented by Mr. W. J. Morris, Bynea. Awards:—

Collection of vegetables: 1, David F. Davies, Pwll; 2, Jabez Thomas, Bynea; 3, W. E. Williams, Tanygraig. Best collection: 1, Jabez Thomas; 2, D. T. Henton, Spitty. Kidney potatoes: 1, W. E. Williams; 2, Jabez Thomas. Round potatoes: 1, David F. Davies; 2, — Beynon, Pwll. Heaviest potato: T. J. Nicholas, Bynea. Runner beans: 1, J. Nicholas, Bynea. Runner beans: 1, — Beynon, Pwll; 2, W. J. Rees, Kidwelly. Stalks of rhubarb: 1, Clifford James, Llwynhendy; 2, Eric Thomas, Berwick Road. Pods of Peas: 1, W. E. Williams; 2, Morgan Jones, Loughor. Carrots (stump): 1, W. J. Rees, Kidwelly; 2, David F. Davies. Carrots (long): 1 and 2, D. T. Henton. Beet (round): 1, John Williams, Burry Port; 2, David F. Davies. Beet (long): 1, Willie Lloyd, Llwynhendy; 2, John Jenkins, Penygraig. Heads of celery: 1, John Jenkins; 2, David F. Davies. Parsnips: 1, John Jenkins; 2, David T. Williams, Soar Road. Leeks: John Jenkins; 2, David. T. Williams. Truss of tomatoes: 1, Eric Thomas; 2, Wm. Reynolds, Llwynhendy. Tomatoes (with stalks): 1 and 2, Eric Thomas. Culinary cabbage (white): 1, W. E. Williams; 2, John Williams. Culinary cabbage (any variety): 1, John Williams; 2, T. J. Nicholas. Bunch of parsley: 1, Jabez Thomas; 2, David F. Davies. Root of parsley: 1, Jabed Thomas. Heads of lettuce: 1, John Jenkins; 2, W. Davies, Gorseinon. Biggest lettuce: John Jenkins. Onions: 1 and 2, Theo. Lewis, Bryn. Onions (novice class): 1, David Reynolds, Llwynhendy; 2, W. E. Williams; 3, D. T. Henton and D. Williams. Pickle onions: 1, Morgan Jones; 2, W. Lloyd. Clumps of shallots: 1, Jabez Thomas; 2, W. E. Williams. Vegetable marrow (yellow): 1, Wm. Reynolds; 2, W. J. Rees; Variegated marrow: David F. Davies; 2, W. E. Williams. Cucumber (indoor): 1, Eric Thomas; 2, Gwilym Williams, Llwynhendy. Culinary apples: 1, John Williams; 2, Gomer Bowen, Bynea. Dessert apples: 1, Gwilym Williams; 2, W. E. Williams. Cooking apples: Jabez Thomas. Culinary pears: 1, W. J. Morris, Bynea; 2, N. Williams, Bynea. Dessert pears: 1 and 2, W. E. Williams. Dish of black currants: 1, John Morgans, Genwen; 2, Gwilym Williams. Dish of gooseberries: 1, George Withey, Bynea; 2, J. Davies, Llangennech. Dish of blackberries: 1 and 2, David F. Davies. Carnations: 1 and 2, A. Evans, Carway. Roses: 1 and 2, Theo. Lewis, Bryn. Pansies: 1, A. Price, Pontyates. Gladioli: 1 and 2, David F. Davies; Cactus dahlias: 1 and 2, John Jenkins. Pom-pom dahlias: 1 and 2, W. E. Williams. Pom-pom dahlias (6 colours): 1 and 2, W. E. Williams. Asters: 1, A. Price; 2, David F. Davies. Antirrhinums: 1, W. E. Williams; 2, A. Evans. Phlox: 1, W. J. Morris 2, Glyn Thomas, Berwick Road. Ten weeks stocks: 1 and 2, John Jenkins. Gent's buttonhole (own foliage rose): 1, Theo. Lewis, Bryn; 2, A. Evans, Carway. Gent's butonhole (own foliage carnation): 1 and 2, A. Evans, Carway. Vase of cut flowers: 1, David F. Davies; 2, A. Evans. Vase of chrysanthemums (out-door): 1 and 2, A. Evans. Sweet peas: 1 and 2, A. Price, Pontyates. Best window plant: 1 and 2, Jabez Thomas. Pot plant (in bloom): 1, Jabez Thomas; 2, John Jenkins. Pot of geraniums: 1 and 2, Jabez Thomas.

RULES AND REGULATIONS OF SHOW.

1.—Exhibitors must provide their own Stands, Boxes and Plates, etc., and all reasonable care will be taken of them, but the Committee will not be responsible for any loss or damage to them, either before, during or after the Exhibition.

2.—All staging MUST be finished by 11 a.m.

3.—The Judges' decisions shall in all cases be final.

4.—No entry whatever will be accepted unless accompanied with full entrance fee, and on the understanding that the Exhibitor abides by these rules.

5.—No exhibit shall be removed from the Show until 6.30. All exhibits must be collected along with a Committeeman.

6.—A protest fee of 5/- must be deposited, with any objections, before 5 p.m. on day of Show, to the Secretary. If protest is found to be frivolous, the protest fee may be forfeited.

7.—No person whatever will be admitted on the morning of Show without a ticket.

8.—Any Exhibitor may enter as many entries as he wishes in any one Class.

9.—No Second Prizes will be awarded if less than three entries are received in each Class.

10.—Rule 7 will be strictly enforced.

AMBULANCE COMPETITION.

Dr. B. D. Hughes Challenge Shield (to be held by winning team for one year).

An Ambulance Competition for the above Challenge Shield, presented for Competition by Dr. B. D. Hughes, Llwynhendy.

Open to Teams of Five Men or Women.

First Prize: The Challenge Shield and	£3 0 0
	£3 0 0
Second Prize	£2 0 0
Third Prize	£1 0 0

The Third Prize will be withheld unless five or more teams compete, and the Second Prize unless more than three teams compete.

Blankets and Stretcher will be provided. Competition will start at 3.0 p.m. prompt.

Entrance Fee, 2/6 per Team, which will include admission to the Horticultural Show, and entries must reach the Secretary not later than August 9th.

Horticultural Show

Will be held at the

RECREATION HALL, BYNEA

And

AMBULANCE COMPETITION

On

SATURDAY, AUGUST 14th, 1943.

Show Open at 1-30 p.m.

Schedule of Classes and Prizes.

Exhibits will be received from 8 a.m. until 11 a.m. morning of Show.

President: W. J. EVANS, Esq., Clifton House, Bynea.
Vice-President: JOHN THOMAS, Esq., Bynea.

Officials:

Chairman of Committee : W. J. MORRIS, Esq., Wilton House, Bynea.
Treasurer : Mr. ANEURIN DAVIES, 4, Saron Road, Bynea.
Joint Secretaries : Mr. JONAH MORRIS, 5, Cwmfelin Row, Bynea.
Mr. JOSEPH DAVIES, Tanygraig, Bynea.
Chief Steward : Mr. W. ROLFE, Waundolybar, Bynea.

ADMISSION Adults, 6d. ; Children, Half-price.

Swansea-Llanelly 'Buses pass within 100 yards of Hall.

Proceeds in aid of the Bynea Soldiers', Sailors' and Airmen's Comforts Fund.

SCHEDULE OF CLASSES AND PRIZES.

Entrance Fee—3d. in Classes 1 to 48.

JUDGES :

Horticulture—Mr. R. DAVIES, Gardener's Lodge, Llanfynydd Road, Carmarthen.

Welsh Cakes.—Mr. WILLIE GRIFFITHS, Bell Stores, Bynea.

VEGETABLE SECTION.

Class No.		Prizes. 1st	2nd
1.—5 Kidney Potatoes (white or coloured)		2/6	1/6
2.—5 Round Potatoes (white or coloured)		2/6	1/6
3.—Bynea Welfare Allotment-holders—5 Potatoes (any variety)		2/6	1/6
4.—For Heaviest Potato in Show		2/6	1/6
5.—6 Runner Beans		2/-	1/-
6.—3 Stalks of Rhubarb		2/6	1/6
7.—6 Pods of Peas		3/-	1/6
8.—3 Carrots		3/6	2/-
9.—3 Beet (Long)		3/-	1/6
10.—3 Beet (Round)		2/6	1/6
11.—2 Heads of Celery		3/6	2/-
12.—3 Parsnips		3/-	1/6
13.—3 Leeks		3/-	1/6
14.—1 Truss of Tomatoes		2/6	1/6
15.—6 Tomatoes (with Stalks attached)		2/6	1/6
16.—2 Culinary Cabbages (white)		2/-	1/-
17.—1 Culinary Cabbage (any variety)		2/-	1/-
18.—1 Bunch of Parsley		2/-	1/-
19.—2 Heads of Lettuce		3/6	2/-
20.—5 Onions		2/6	1/6
21.—5 Onions (Novice Class) (not won 1st Prize on Onions)		2/6	1/6
22.—4 Shallots		2/-	1/-
23.—1 Vegetable Marrow		2/6	1/-

FRUIT SECTION.

24.—5 Culinary Apples		2/6	1/6
25.—5 Dessert Apples		2/6	1/6
26.—1 Cooking Apple		2/-	1/-
27.—5 Pears		2/6	1/6
28.—Dish of Black Currants		2/-	1/-
29.—Dish of Red or White Currants		2/-	1/-
30.—Dish of Gooseberries		2/-	1/-

FLOWER SECTION.

31.—6 Carnations, Border (not less than 3 colours), to be shown in a Vase		3/-	2/-
32.—3 Carnations, Perpetuals		2/-	1/-
33.—6 Roses (not less than 3 colours)		2/6	1/6
34.—3 Gladioli (not less than 3 colours)		2/6	1/6
35.—6 Cactus Dahlias (not less than 3 colours)		2/6	1/6

FLOWER SECTION.—Continued.		Prizes. 1st	2nd
Class No.			
36.—9 Cactus Dahlias (not less than 6 colours)		5/-	2/6
37.—6 Decorative Dahlias (not less than 3 colours)		2/6	1/6
38.—6 Pom-Pom Dahlias (not less than 3 colours)		3/-	2/-
39.—6 Asters		2/6	1/6
40.—Antirrhinums (6 blooms, 3 colours)		2/6	1/6
41.—Phlox (3 vases, 1 spray in each, 3 colours)		2/6	1/6
42.—Ten-week Stocks (3 spikes, different colours)		2/6	1/6
43.—Gent's Buttonhole		2/6	1/6
44.—Vase of Cut Flowers (not less than 6 colours)		3/-	1/6
45.—Sweet Peas (1 vase, 12 stems, not less than 3 colours)		2/6	1/6
46.—Best Window Plant		2/6	1/6
47.—Pot Plant (in bloom)		2/-	1/-
48.—1 Vase of Chrysanthemums (out-door)			

A **Silver Cup**, kindly presented by W. J. Morris, Esq., Bynea, for most number of points from Class 1—48 (except Class 3). The Cup to be won three times, not necessarily in successive years. Points to be awarded as follows :—First, 2 points : Second, 1 point.

Winner for 1941 and 1942 : Mr. Willie Phillips, Pwll.

CLASSES FOR SCHOOLCHILDREN.

(Under 14 years of age). Entrance Free.

(Area : Bynea, Bryn and Llwynhendy).

49.—Best 4 Potatoes (any colour or shape)		2/6	1/6
50.—1 Bunch of Calendulas or Old English Marigolds		2/6	1/6
51.—Longest String of White Butterflies		2/-	1/-

(Prizes for Classes 49 and 50 kindly given by W. J. Morris, Esq., Bynea).

WELSH CAKES.

Entrance Fee 3d.

52.—6 Welsh Cakes		2/6	1/6

COLLECTION OF VEGETABLES.

53.—Best Collection of Vegetables (open) :

1st Prize, £1 5s. 6d. ; 2nd Prize, 10/- ; 3rd Prize, 5/-. Entrance Fee, 1/-. Space allowed, 3 ft.

Entries for the Open Collection to be in the hands of the Secretary not later than August 12th.

54.—Best Collection : 2 Beet, 2 Potatoes, 2 Onions, 2 Carrots, 2 Parsnips, 1 Cabbage. 1st Prize, 7/6 ; 2nd Prize, 3/6. Entrance Fee, 6d.

BYNEA GARDEN AND ALLOTMENT ASSOCIATION CLASSES.

	Prizes. 1st	2nd
3 Beet	2/6	1/3
3 Carrots	2/6	1/3
Onions	2/6	1/3
Potatoes	2/6	1/3
Cabbages	2/6	1/3

This Class is confined to Members of the Bynea Garden and Allotment Association who have had their Seeds and Potatoes through the Association.

The Incline is the continuation of Saron Road which leads to the Genwen.

The stream would flow from Penygraig down Parc Richard and would continue to Nantwen. Eventually forming a natural waterfall into Bynea quarry (Genwen quarry).

Maggie's Chip Shop

Whenever one thinks of Bynea there is one place that is dear to every ones heart - 'Maggie's Chip Shop' - it was popular with young and old. The chip shop was run by three spinsters, Gwynneth, Gertie and Maggie Jones who lived in the little cottages in Bevan's Row a few yards from the shop.

The shop was open every night except on a Sunday and every evening you would see Gertie walk back and fore with the bucket of potatoes ready for Gwynneth to chip with their hand operated chipping machine. Near the side window would sit Maggie stoking the fire that cooked the chips, and it was she that always served the chips.

There was a little side window where Maggie stoked her fryer, and the curtain was always half open so that she could survey the outside world while she went about her work.

The benches that we sat on while we waited to be served would be set around the wall, and these would have been scrubbed until white, and immaculately clean. There would always be clean sawdust on the floor and as children we loved to shuffle our feet in it to make patterns.

Bynea Park

The park was the Jewel of Bynea. It was a well laid out 2 acres of land with a Pavilion and a two gated entrance. The outer paths around the perimeter had bench seats every 50 yards. There was a central path leaving two sides of flower beds in each half (see drawing).

In the early Thirties it was well kept by village volunteers and it was rated the best park in the Llanelli area. When the War came and all the able men were called up, the Elders of the village seem to loose interest and the children would play Tarzan over the trees, breaking them in the process and soon it became into disrepair.

The planting of flowers ceased and like all the redundant old buildings of the previous industries it became dilapidated. The only area to survive was the old sand pit and the park field which was constantly in use every evening. All the children would gather together to select sides for either cricket or rugby.

The park committee was eventually disbanded and it was eventually given to the Bynea Rugby Club to be turned into their existing pitches.

Terry Davies. 2010

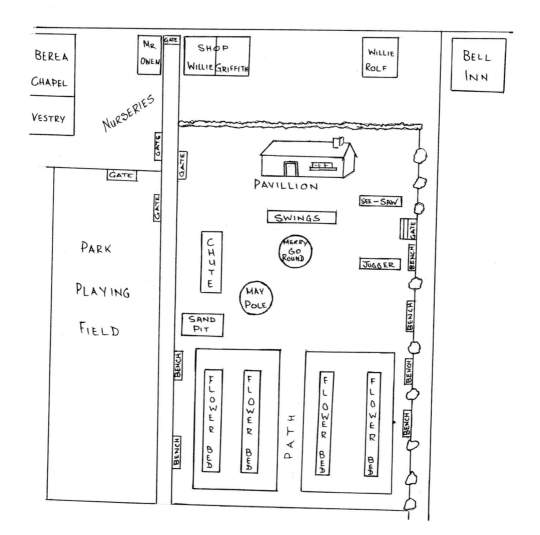

BEREA
CHAPEL
VESTRY

NURSERIES

MR OWEN

GATE

SHOP
WILLIE GRIFFITH

WILLIE ROLF

BELL INN

GATE

GATE

GATE

GATE

PARK

PLAYING

FIELD

PAVILLION

SEE-SAW

SWINGS

CHUTE

MERRY GO ROUND

JUGGER

GATE

BENCH

MAY POLE

BENCH

SAND PIT

BENCH

BENCH

BENCH

FLOWER BED

FLOWER BED

PATH

FLOWER BED

FLOWER BED

BENCH

Dedwyddwch y Plant ar Barc y Bynea

Mi welais y plant yn y tywod,
Gwneud cestyll a thwr ar bob llaw,
Mor ddedwydd yr cofio a chanu
Heb dyfroedd yr afon na glaw

Edrychais o'u hamgylch - er syndod
R'oedd seddau o'u cylch yr un modd,
I bawb sydd yn dewis cael gorffwys
Ac enwau pob un wrth ei rodd

O'u cwmpas mae blodau amrywiol
A llawer i eneth fach dwt
Yn dringo i fyny y grisiau
Ac yna i lawr dros y shwt

Beth arall sydd eisiau, dywedwch?
Cewch Maypole, nei Swing yn eich tro;
Amynedd sydd eisiau gyfeillion,
Mae gwledd oedd ar ben y See So.

Y cyfan sydd wedi ei wneuthi'r,
Diogelwch y plant ydyw'r nod;
Ond 'chydig er hynny sy'n gweithio -
Mae llawer yn mynd ac yn dod.

Beth bynnag sydd eto
I ddyfod Rhaid talu am bopeth a ddaw;
Am hynny cewch eisteddfod yn fuan,
A chroeso a'r docyn bob llaw.

W. J. Morris.

Pafiliwn Bach Parc y Bynea

Adeiliad bach tlws yw'r pafiliwn,
A phawb yn ei hoffi yn fawr;
Mae lle i'r cardotyn sy'n crwydro
Gael hamdden ac eistedd i lawr.

Rwy'n cofio'r hen fangre'n anialwch,
Heb flodyn, ond briaill ar berth;
Mae heddiw'n baradwys i chwarae.
I blant a hen ffrindiau gael nerth.

Teyrngarwch amynedd cyfeillion,
A chalon bob amser i'r gwaith,
Sy'n amlwg i bawb sydd yn dyfod
Er cysur i ddyn ar ei daith

Hyfrydwch bob amser yw uno,
Beth bynnag yw'r rhwystr fe ddaw
Ffyddlondeb diflino, mae'n sicr
A digon o weithwyr wrth law

Rhowd araith ar freuddwyd hen
Frenin A'i deulu y modd 'roedd yn byw
A'r Ethiop sydd heddiw yn griddfan
Am ryddid addoli ei Dduw.

Bu hanes am Rwsia a'r Pabydd,
A hanes y pentre a fu,
Gan frodyr talentog yr ardal,
A dyna sy'n gysur i ni

Mae rhyddid i unrhyw bererin,
Os teimla roi'i araith yn rhad;
Bydd croeso'r Pafiliwn, mi gredaf,
Yn ddigon o dal a mwynhad.

Nos Wener yw 'r noson ddelfrydol
I ddechrau yn union am saith;
Os methir a bod yno'n brydlon, Rhaid
dychwel yn ol ar eich taith.

Mi garwn gael uno'r gymdogaeth
I godi adeilad o faint,
Er cynnal cyngherddau'r eglwysi
Fo'n urddas i'r ardal a braint

William John Morris Bynea

Min-y-Graig Nurseries

These nurseries were owned by Mr David/ Dafydd Owen, and after his death the nurseries were taken over by his son Mr Evan William Owen. It was a busy, demanding business where family members were involved. Due to demand of fresh produce of tomatoes, cucumbers, and grapes, they would go around the village with their baskets of these lovely produce.

Onions would be grown from seeds and sold as established plants by the hundreds, they were in great demand. Many varieties of flowers were grown, but all had to be suitable for making wreaths, on occasions orders would be so large that they would be working all night to meet demands.

During the war years, a coal allowance was given to Mr Owen, in order to heat the greenhouses. There were three very large and two smaller ones, which were built by his son-in-law David Wynne, these were all heated by coal. Immediately at the sound of the siren these coal fires had to be shuttered off to eliminate any visible light for enemy aircraft.

In order to assist with food production during the war years 1939 1945, Mr. Owen was given six months dispensation from his Home Guard duties.

This portion of land was cultivated for growing vegetables and flowers, which were in great demand by villagers. Ground rent for this plot was £4-4s-0p in 1919. It was converted to Bynea Park playing field.

TELEPHONE: 150.

UPLANDS,
NEAR LLANELLY.

September 16th 1932.

Mr David Owen,
Wsundolybar
Cwmfelin. Bynea.

Dear Sir,

I have to formally notify you that I have sold the land occupied by your garden to the Bynea Childrens Welfare Trustees. This sale is subject to the existing tenancy and I have pointed out to the Secretary that if occupation of any portion of the ground in your occupation is required by the Welfare, they must first of all obtain your consent & any compensation required would have to be paid to you.

The rental will be due to the Estate up to the date of completion of which I will advise you in due course.

I do not know what arrangements you may make with the Trustees but in so far as the Estate is concerned I shall be satisfied to consider it's termination on the 29th inst if this is agreeable to yourself,

Yours truly,

RAF Pencoed Works

During the War the works became an aeroplane recycling plant, where crashed and damaged air planes were transported from all over the country to be cannibalised for reusable parts to be used for spares for the existing fleet of planes.

There were Spitfires and Hurricanes and Lockhead Lightnings with lightweight bodies made out of ply wood so that they could boost their speed to 'out run' the German planes. The Lockhead Lightening was usually used for reconnaissance flights or photographing bomb damage of German targets.

What a playground for us children. We would sit in the cockpits of these planes and dream of shooting down the Luftwaffe planes. We would then take a piece of the Perspex wind screen and make rings for our fingers out of them they became precious mementos as we had never seen Perspex before. There was great excitement, 3 Sunderland Flying boats had arrived, and they were floating in the reed bed area at the back of the works, their long bodies raised on floats. The playing in the planes came to an abrupt end one day when a finger and thumb that were very black were found on the floor of a plane. We never played there again.

At the end of the War there would be truck loads of guns, rifles and hand guns all confiscated from the Germans. There were helmets by the dozen, and then came the Japanese swords with Ruby encrusted hilts. Suddenly we became pirates duelling with these Japanese swords. All the guns had been decommissioned and they were put into steam press and squeezed into a large block.

Terry Davies 2010

Yr Ychydig Ffyddlon

Wn i ddim os ydych chwi wedi sylwi
Wrth fynychu oedfaon fel hyn
Pa mor rhyfedd o ffyddlon yw'r gwragedd
Tra mae'r dynion yn llawer mwy prin
Mae 'run fath mewn Cymanfa Ganu,
Neu gyngerdd , neu Gyrddau Mawr,
Y gwragedd, sy'n parhau yn ffyddlon
Does ddim llawer o ddynion i'w gweld nawr.
Ond sut mae hyn wedi digwydd
Pam newid y ffordd o fyw
Ydy dynion wedi colli diddordeb-
Mewn crefydd a Beibil, a Duw?
Ydi nhw'n credu mae rhywbeth i'r gwragedd
Yw cerdded y llwybyr cul
Ac yn meddwl, ar ôl prynhawn Sadwrn
Mae diwrnod ymlacio yw'r Sul?
O do, mi arhosodd y gwragedd hyd y diwedd
Hyd y death E o'i boenau yn rhydd
A'r gwragedd oedd yno gynta
Pan wawriodd y trydydd dydd.
Ac felly, nid rhyfedd eu gweled nhw heddiw
Yn parhau i fod yn ffyddlon i'r cwrdd
Tra bod y rhan fwyaf o'r dynion
Yn dewis cadw i ffwrdd.
Ac i chwi y gwragedd mae'r diolch
Am gadw'n addoldai yn fyw
Ac os na gewch chwi barch gyda dynion
I chwi'n sicir o'i gael gyda Duw.
Ac mi ddaliwn i drwy'r cyfan i gredu
Fod na derfyn ar bopeth sy'n ffôl
Ac mae yna arwyddion, hyd yn oed heddiw
Fod y llanw ar fin dod yn ôl

Wel, wedi dweud yna, ni allaf byth ac anghofio'r blynyddoedd cynta pan y deuthum i Berea, nôs Sadwrn cynta y Cyrddau Mawr, a'r Capel dan ei sang a minnau'n rhoi cymorth i gario seddau a ffwrymau i'r alai, o'r fath olygfa! Ac o'r fath ganu gwefreiddiol! Beth sydd

wedi digwydd dwedwch? Wel, gan fod un droed, megys, gennyf ar ddechrau'r ganrif a'r llall bron ar ei diwedd,mi wnaf fy ngorau i ateb. Beth yw achos y dirywiad? Wel, yn blwmp ac yn blaen- rhieni gwael, cartrefi gwael, ac esiampl wael i'w plant, mewn gwirionedd, rhieni ddim yn deilwng i gael plant. Wel, paham meddech chi, fod rhieni yn ymddwyn felly? Wel eto, mi gredwn i, mi ddechreuodd y dirywiad yn ystod y Rhyfel Mawr diwethaf, pan aeth y mamau i'r ffatrioedd i weithio, a chael blâs y 'pay packet'.Cyn hynny, tebyg mae'r gŵr neu'r tad oedd yn mynd allan ar nôs Sadwrn am ei beint, ond ar ôl hyn, dyma'r fam hefyd yn mofyn ei `night out`. Ond, beth am eu plant? Wel, mae nhw'n cael eu bwyd, efallai, a'u 'pocket money'(swm sylweddol weithiau),ond sylwch, mae yna un peth mawr yn eisiau,does dim cariad mwyach yn y cartref, a dyna un peth sy'n hanfodol i blentyn. Y peth sydd yn dilyn wedyn yw fod y plant yma yn crynhoi ar gorneli'r strydoedd ac yn chwilio am ryw ddifyrwch a hwnnw yn arwain yn fynych iawn i ddistryw a'r plant yma yw ein dinasyddion ni heddiw a dyna achos y picil i ni ynddo y dyddiau hyn.

Bryn Davies, Heol Hen. Diacon yn Capel Berea.

Côr Capel Berea, 1954?
Gweinidog y Parchedig R. Edwards a'i Arweinydd Mr. Fred Evans.

The British Legion

The British Legion in Bynea has stood at the top of the hill going out (or coming in, whichever way you are travelling) of the village for many years and can be said to be the last (or first) building of importance in the life of the Bynea people.

Bynea and Llwynhendy members of the Legion who still march to St. David's Church on Remembrance Sunday, where they present wreathes with great pride for their fellow comrades.

A few yards opposite the British Legion was the old Blacksmith in years gone by.

Part Three
Introduction

We have now left the village of Bynea with its rich historical background. We are now entering her sister village of Llwynhendy. If it wasn't for the sign at the side of the road one wouldn't be aware of the fact, as they blend in so well together. This area also has strong industrial roots with Trostre (now Corus) near by. Like Bynea, Llwynhendy has also seen many changes throughout the years.

Soar Chapel, Llwynhendy

Changing times and a changing community of residents in the Llwynhendy area, means that there are many who are unable to speak or understand Welsh. Soar Chapel, totally Welsh for over one hundred and fifty years, has responded to the need by offering services in English on the third Sunday of each month, with a warm welcome assured to all who are interested in attending.

Regular worshippers has ensured that the venture is a success.

Marian Williams 2010

Are you in this photograph taken at Soar, Llwynhendy during a concert at the Chapel in 1954.

Soar Chapels children's choir taken in 1968.

Members and friends of Soar Chapel taking part in a drama, 'The Choice', based on the story of Easter.

Penygraig

The village of Penygraig stands high overlooking Bynea and Llwynhendy, with panoramic views of Loughor river and estuary on to the Gower peninsula, Whiteford lighthouse, which is a cast iron lighthouse, then Trostre tinplate works, Machynys, and the Goalposts, newly placed on Berwick roundabout.

Penygraig is part of the Gerald of Wales Trail, which crossed the River Loughor, walking over farmland; placing stones at approximately every 200 yards, to mark the Pilgrims Way, these landmarks have now disappeared. They continued through Pencoed, Penygraig, down to Soar Road, Paradise Row, until they came to Capel Dewi, a Chapel of Ease, where part of the ruins remain today. This area was an ancient burial ground; unfortunately this is now under the road where St. David's Church stands today.

Penygraig above Soar Chapel, with panoramic views, May 2010.

The village of Bynea from Penygraig.

HIRAETH

Yn fy Meddwl Pan ddawr Hirnos
Ar Benygraig yr wyf yn aros
Wrth fy gefn mae y bwthyn
Lle le magwyd fi yn blentyn
Yno mae fy mam annwyl eto
Gwraig yn weddw methu cyffro
Cofio rwyf am hi o hyd
Am chwiorydd yn y cartref clyd
Wrth fy nraed mi welaf Bynea
Dros y bont fferm fach y Glynea
Rhodion llygad dros y meisydd
Fferm y Berwig fferm Benclacwydd
Bellach wel y Goder fechan
Yr afon Llwchwr yn dawel llifan
Hen Benclawdd yn yr Haul yn gwenu
Swn asyn ar yr awel yn brefu

Gwelaf eto yr goleudy
Ar y tywod ger bron Llanelli
Troi if chwyth mi wel yr eglwys
Ar bryn bach y Llwchwr yn aros
Swn ei clychau dod imi'n dawel
Cario'n naeth ar fron yr awel
Ac ei ton fel geiriau hapaus
Dywed imi paid bod'n ofnus

Hiraeth sydd yn llenwi fy galon
Cofio cartref ar teulu dirion
Daw yr amser fydd ny heddwch
Ar y ddaear mae nawr gymisgwch
Hiraeth ddaw i gwrdd dyn goreu
felly ar ol nos y boreu
Tro dy ben a cer i gysgu
Fydd di'n teimlo'n well yfori.

J. H. Harold

The Poem 'Hiraeth' was written by J. H. Harold, whilst serving in North Africa during the Second World War. The sketch accompanying the poem is that of the cottage that he lived in, in Penygraig. He mentions in the poem the view from Penygraig looking down on Bynea, Llwynhendy and Llanelli and his longing for home.

The Ship Inn, 1940's.

The Ship Inn

Trading began at the Ship Inn during the late 1800's. It was then known as the 'Old Ship Inn'. Buckley's Brewery were the owners, but the land was leased from the Stepney family of Llanelli. The tenants had to pay rent for the premises and also a yearly ground rent payment.

In 1929 Gwladys and Gustave Kleinsmith took over the tenancy. In January 1932 tragedy struck, when their eldest son, 18 years old, Jonathan was killed. An outside retaining garden wall collapsed and fell on him.

Mrs Kleinsmith was well known in the area for her healing oils and ointment. People came from near and far to be treated. Her ointment, used as a cure for all types of skin complaints was known locally as 'ELIGWYN' The recipe has been passed down from generation to generation within the immediate family and is still made to-day. Mrs Kleinsmith died in 1949 and her husband and family left the Ship Inn in 1953 New people took over the tenancy, but the 'pub' ceased trading in the late 1960's. The building was completely renovated and is now a private dwelling house.

Eiryl Williams (nee Dykes)

Eliseralis

People from all walks of life would also purchase 'Eli Seralice' an ointment similar to Mrs Kleinsmith's 'Eligwyn'. This lady lived in Cwmfelin Road.

Facts

When things began to get heated at 'The Ship Inn' on Saturday nights after the clients had a few drinks, Marie, Mrs Kleinsmith's daughter would calm things down by introducing a few facts to take their minds off drinking. There were numerous facts - dealing with local and world wide topics. Marie often said that the 'facts' saved many a 'punch-up' Here are some examples of the facts that Marie wrote down about Bynea and Llwynhendy and the Llanelli area:

St. David's Church Llwynhendy was opened in 1882.
The widening of Llwynhendy Road near Ship Inn started 5th December 1933
when Mrs Wilson's shop and cottage called 'Cornwrdd' were demolished
David Thomas Ship Inn opened his premises on 6th May 1914.

Bynea School opened May 7th 1898

Explosion at Pwll Pencoed Bynea 18th September 1901 - 1 killed.

Llanelli trams started in 1911, and ended 16th January 1933.

Llanelli trolley buses started on Bynea & Loughor route 26th December 1932, ended 8th November 1952.

Llanelli Town Hall opened 31st March 1896

Llanelli General Hospital opened in 1885

Llanelli Synagogue opened in May 1909

Llanelli National Choir sang before King Edward VI on the Royal Yacht at Cardiff Docks 20th June 1907

A dangerous fire broke out in a house in Felinfoel, Llanelli, on 23rd February 1928. Four lives were lost.

Parc Howard Llanelli opened 21st September 1912, an area of 28 acres.

The first train passed over Llanelli- Llandeilo railway on 15th January 1857.

The anniversary at St Peter's Hall Llanelli was on the 22nd October 1939. It being 70 years old built in 1869.

Mabon unveiled at Llanelli a memorial to Tom Phillips Tinplate Leader on 15th January 1906.

Springbox paid their visit to Llanelli 1906/7. Llanelli won 2 goals, Penalty & a Try. Revisited in 1912.

Llanelli town was raised to be Borough on 14th August 1913.

Lady Howard Stepney was honoured to be the Freeman of Llanelli 21 years later 14th August 1934, the 5th Freeman, Mr Evan Jones, Bynea, celebrated his 94th birthday on Monday 22nd June 1935. He remembered the days when the railway came no further than Swansea, and people had to walk 12 miles to catch a train.

The last payment for schools was on August 31st 1891.

Mr B Williams finished boot repair business at the Ship Inn, Llwynhendy, on February 20th 1933.

The Old Chapel Fair, Llwynhendy, first opened in 1509.

Marie collected many more, but they are too numerous to refer to here.

St. Davids Church, Llwynhendy

The present Church was erected in 1882 and opened on Tuesday, 26th April in that year, being dedicated to St. David the Patron Saint of Wales. It was built on part of the site of a former 12th Century Church, part of the ruins of which are still visible. The new Church was built at a total cost of £500 which was raised by subscription. In 1926 a Church hall was built on the opposite side of the road and was well used over the years but, sadly, had to be demolished in 2005 having become unsafe.

In 1939 the Church was closed for renovation works including provision of the Chancel step and the Altar step, addition of the Porch and interior decoration. The Re-Opening Service was held on 7th November 1939 at which the then Reverend Lord Bishop of St. David's presided when many. Memorial Gifts were dedicated. The beautiful stained-glass window behind the Altar, depicting 'The Good Shepherd' was dedicated on 17th December 1939 and promptly 'boarded up' for the duration of the War to preserve it from probable damage during the hostilities. The Church was Licensed for Marriages in 1939.

Between 1967 and 1978 a new pipe organ was installed, the Church was re-decorated and re-carpeted, the Bell was re-tuned and the Lychgate erected.

The Church's Centenary was celebrated on Sunday, 25th April 1982 and Memorial Gifts were dedicated by The Lord Bishop of St. David's, the Rt.Rev'd George Noakes. On the following Monday and Wednesday the pageant 'The Light-bearers of Wales' was performed by members of the Choir, Sunday School scholars and Church Officers, who were trained by the Rev'd Angela Gray with support from Mrs Sheila Davies and Mrs Merrill Thomas. The Church was filled on both occasions and was deemed by all to have been an impressive production; as a reward the children were given a celebratory party at the end of the week. A Flower Festival was held in the July and during this Centenary year several former Vicars and Curates returned to the Church to Preach at various services.

A little while before the Centenary a new wooden ceiling was installed in the Church of a rich-coloured Parana Pine, adding to the beauty of this little gem of a church. It still glows richly today.

The 125th Anniversary was celebrated on Sunday, 22nd April 2007 when a new Altar and other Memorial Gifts were dedicated by The Lord Bishop of St David's, the Rt. Rev'd Carl Cooper. Celebrations continued with a Flower Festival and a week of events between 22nd and 28th April and followed by a Confirmation Service on 3rd May celebrated by The Lord Bishop.

Over the years the Church has been served by numerous Vicars and Curates of whom the present Vicar, the Reverend Canon Angela M. Gray, has served the longest - firstly as Deaconess, then Deacon, Deacon-in-Charge and currently as Vicar - over a period of 30 years.

We still have a very strong Mothers' Union Branch which meets in Church once a month.

Margaret Robinson, June 2010

St. David's Church, Llwynhendy.

Tea time at St. David's Church hall sometime during the 1950's.

1st St. David's Llwynhendy, Brownies 1984
L/R back row - Alison Watkins, Merle Davies, Nina Tudor, Peggy Norris and Mrs E. Clarke.

L/R Mrs Susan Williams, Club Leader, Mr Vernon Griffith, Mr Huw Bevan, Mr Couldrey,
Rt. Rev. Bishop George Noakes, Rev Angela Gray, Rev. John Byron Davies, Father Barnabus, Orthodox Priest,
Mr Gerald Clement, Mr Harry Jones and the Llwynhendy Cubs Group.

Centenary Celebrations
Pageant - the light bearers of Wales, April 1982

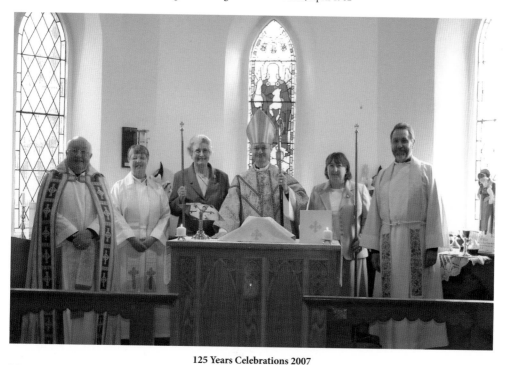

125 Years Celebrations 2007
L/R: Venerable Alun Evans, Archdeacon of Carmarthen, Rev. Canon Angela Gray, Mrs Margaret Robinson, Church Warden, Rt. Rev. Bishop Carl Cooper, Mrs Barbara Anthony, Church Warden, Rev. Huw James, Area Dean of Kidwelly.

*The following gifts have been presented and gratefully
accepted by the Church for its 125th Anniversary and
Will be dedicated by the Lord Bishop of St. Davids
The Right Reverend Carl Cooper*

ALTAR

In memory of Dr Roland Charles Gwillim Hughes.
The gift of his family.

MEMORIAL BOOKCASE

In memory of Mair Robinson.
The gift of her husband Sidney Robinson

MEMORIAL BOOK

In memory of Joyce Evans.
The gift of her family.

ALTAR BOOK - "THE HOLY EUCHARIST"

In memory of Richard Anthony Roberts.
The gift of his family.

ALTAR BOOK - "THE NEW CALENDAR AND THE COLLECTS"

In memory of William Hugh Thomas.
The gift of his family.

Ardal Bynea a Llwynhendy

Ardal gweithwyr tun a dur, a choliers a cychydig bach o wahaniaeth mewn iaith hefyd (gwir y fe's fel y dywed pobol o'r tu allan) yw Bynea a Llwynhendy. Dyma i chi enghraifft fechan:-

Ar y Ffôn

Helo Lisi fach, fe sy na, jiw mae lais e i glywed yn od ochor hyn
Mae'n siwr fod vandals wedi mesan â'r thing
Wel, gwedw wrtho i nawr sut mae pethe da fe
Odi pethe fe'n gwbod, yn weddol o'i lle?
Odi mam ei wr e yn fyw o hyd
Waeth oedd hi ddim yn un o'r rhai goreuon y byd?
`Beth wedws e, wedi priodi, wel "Jiw, Jiw",
Pwy oedd y nyt a ddaliodd y scriw?
Ta pwy oedd y dyn bach, mae'n siwr o ddyfaru
Waeth oedd hi ddim o'r teip allse dyn ei charu
Ond na fe, beth yr ots, ma fe Lisi fach wedi cael gwaredigaeth
Beth? Beth mae fe'n dweud, pwy `news` sydd geni ffordd hyn?
Wel `does fawr am wn i i'w hala fe'n syn
O, fe'n gwbod Jane Ann No.4 Penceilogi,
Wel, ei chwaer Sali Sue, mae wedi priodi
Fe'n gwbod roedd i lawr sha San Clêr, morwyn mewn plâs
A ma nhw'n dweud bod hi'n gorffod, wel na beth cas
A fe'n gwybod am Raymond wrth gwrs, ma fe'n perthyn yn agos
Mae e wedi gwneud ffortiwn wrth werthi tomatoes
Mae na siarad for hyn, p'un ai gwir neu peidio,
Fod e'n symud i blâs sha ochor Llandeilo.
Wel, Lis fach, mae'r pishin dwy geiniog hyn nawr ar ben
A gwell nawr mewn pryd fydd dwedyd amen:
Nawr cofiw fe ffono, os aiff rhyw beth yn rong
Rwy'n mynd nawr te Lis fach, "so long"

Wel, rhywbeth tebyg i yna oedd y siarad i'w glywed i ddyn newydd i'r cylch.

Bryn Davies, Heol Hen

Llwyn Hall

These are only two of the many bills that were found in one of the chimneys at Llwynhall by the late Richard Burrows during renovations. These bills reflect on the life of Mr John Humphreys whilst he lived at Llwynhall (Maes yr Haf was originally the name of the house).

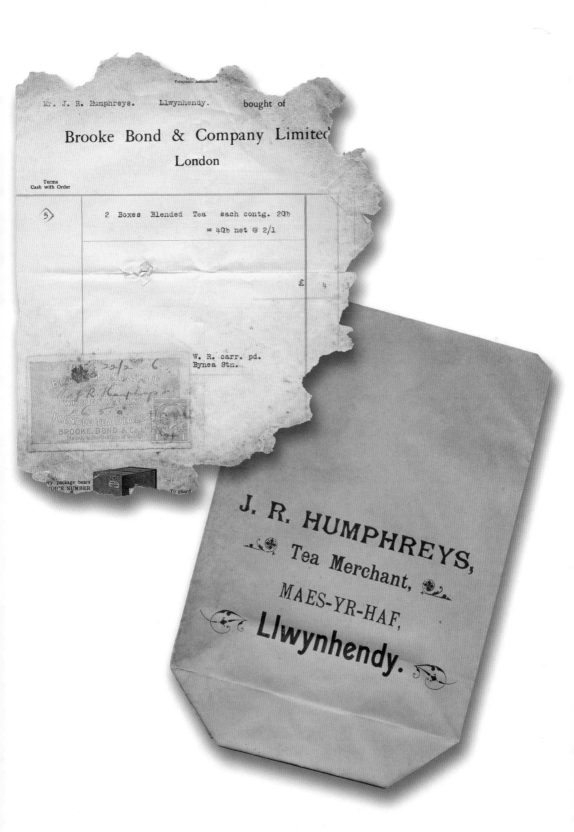

Mr. J. R. Humphreys.   Llwynhendy.   bought of

Brooke Bond & Company Limited
London

Terms
Cash with Order

| 5 | 2 Boxes Blended Tea   each contg. 20℔ = 40℔ net @ 2/1 | | £ 4 3 |

W. R. carr. pd.
Bynea Stn.

J. R. HUMPHREYS,
Tea Merchant,
MAES-YR-HAF,
Llwynhendy.

"Llwyn Hall"

WORDS BY JOHN R. HUMPHREYS.

MUSIC BY FRED EVANS, Llwynhendy.

The Saviour's Call

I hear Thy voice, O Lord, 'tis calling me,
O give me faith to rise and follow Thee;
Like Thy disciples on that distant shore,
Obey Thy call, and follow evermore.

I hear Thy call in Nature every day,
From gentle dawn that comes to light my way,
Until the sun is setting in the West
To give my tired lids their nightly rest.

Thy call is in the flower that telleth me,
That for my sake it smiles so tenderly;
Thy call is in the beauty of the trees,
It whispers softly in their rustling leaves.

Mountains and vales, and sapphire stars above,
In silence call to me to see Thy love;
Whilst rivers and the seas rehearse Thy praise,
And call my soul to worship all my days.

Yet God in nature is too far away
To save my soul; I must have Christ to say
" Come, follow me, and I will give you rest,
" I'll cleanse thy soul, and you'll be ever blest."

Our Lane

The little lane that leads to home,
Is beautiful to-day;
Hedges bedecked with hawthorn buds-
Drooping with jewelled spray.

In rain it is a silvered lane,
Skirting in vivid green;
Tall elms like sentinels stand up,
Making a pleasing scene.

On sunny days 'tis all alive
With boys and girls at play;
We witness childhood's innocence-
Rememb'ring many a day

Along its verge are pleasant farms,
Those hives of industry;
We hear the farmyard friendly sounds-
Peculiar melody.

Bordered are homes of Erwlas,
Ddolfawr and village store;
Cottages, where the miller once
 With white coat reigned of yore.

When sunset blushes in the West
And daylight on the wane:
'Tis then a favourite evening walk-
Our village Lover's Lane

Throughout the happy fleeting years,
We've watched each day's routine,
From milk-carts patter after dawn,
'Till night-time's closing scene.

Ah! Someone loved this little lane,
I learnt to love it too;
And for her sake I'll hold it dear,
Until this life is through.

This poem was written by Mrs Humphreys `Llwynhall` looking down the lane to 'The Bridges' - 'Y Bontydd'

At Llwynhall we now venture right, up towards the village of Llwynhendy, passing the old familiar site of the magnificent building known to everyone as Nazareth Methodist Chapel. Truly a magnificent building in its hey day. It opened its doors on November 5th 1927, but sadly like so many of our chapels these days it had to close on December 27th 2009.

It was an unforgettable morning however for those who attended the last morning communion that was conducted by Rev. Eifion Roberts, and the service was followed with welcoming refreshments whilst those present were able to talk about old times, and say 'goodbye' to the old familiar surroundings.

The photographs are those that were taken of the chapel children who performed a Nativity Play sometime in the 1950's, and also a tea party that was held for the children and the adults of Nazareth around 1945 1947.

If you were there when the photographs of the tea parties were taken perhaps you could let the owner of the photographs know by leaving a message at the Red Cow in Bynea.

At the end of the steep hill we come to the end of the road, and the old Llwynhendy school, that was opened in 1870 by the Llanelli School Board. However, the building is now used as a thriving Community Centre, and serves the community with day and evening classes for adults, Youth clubs, and 'Ti a Fi' Welsh pre-school classes. This was the first Community Centre to be opened in Carmarthenshire.

Llwynhendy Infant Welfare Centre.

Coronation Tea — 16th June 1953.

Donations received.

For Food.
Mrs Richards. 5/-.
Mrs Victor Thomas. 5/-.
Mrs Davies, Bon Vue 9/- — 19/-

For Ice Cream
Mrs Sale 10/-
Mrs Gordon Thomas 5/-
Mrs Jones, Police Station 5/-
Mrs Morris, Hawthorn 5/-
Mrs Richards 5/-
Mrs White 5/-
Mrs G. W. Thomas 5/- — £2-0-0
                        £2-19-0

E Richards
20.10.53

Sale of Food.
Mrs Gordon Thomas. 1/3.
Mrs White 4/4
Mrs Morris 5/-
Mrs Joshua 3/-
Mrs Ed. Evans 6/2½
Mrs Jones Police Stat. -/6
Mrs Tucher Jones 4/10
Mrs G. W. Thomas 6/6.
Mrs Richards -/9 £1.10.4½

Amounts Paid out.
Mrs Jones. Cleaner 10/-.
Mr Marchesine (Ice Cream) £1.13/-.
For Comets (parties & buns) 6/-
For Iced Cake to Mrs Morris £1.1/6 £3-16-6.

Cash Statement
By Donations £2-19-0
By Sale of Food 1-10-4½
        Total £4-9-4½
Amount paid out 3-16-6.

'Vechtra' German Exchange visit 1955/56 taken at the back of Llwynhendy community centre. M. Bonurelli.

Part Four
Llwynhendy School

Did you attend Llwynhendy School when these photographs were taken in 1961 and 1981?

Llwynhendy School - trip to London during Coronation Year 1953.

Bryn Teg Primary School

Bryn Teg primary school was created because of the amalgamation of Llwynhendy Junior school and Ysgol Yr Ynys Nursery/Infant school in September 2005. Initially the school was based at the Ysgol Yr Ynys site where 3 extra classrooms (porta cabins) were brought in to accommodate the extra children.

The Junior school in Trallwm road, Llwynhendy was knocked down and there was a tremendous amount of excavation work undertaken and gradually the new Ysgol Bryn Teg was built. Children and staff moved into the state of the art building on the 5th September 2008. The first Headteacher, who has been responsible for the amalgamation and the move into new premises is Mrs Delyth Williams.

Llys enwau rhai o Drigolion Llwynhendy
Nicknames of some Llwynhendy characters

Wel nawr am ychydig, wnewch chwi ymdawelu
Gan wrando a chofio am hen ardal Llwynhendy
Hen enwau sydd gennym, llysenwau pobol
O'r dyddiau cynt i lawr i'r presennol
Rhai enw gwych, a rhai enwau garw
Rhai yn fyw heddiw, a rhai wedi marw
Dydw i yn bersonol ddim yn nabod nhw i gyd
Waeth dyn bach dwad ydw i rhan hyn o'r byd
Ond ta waeth am hynny, mae'r enwau ar glawr
Ac heb ragor o siarad, mi dechreua i nawr

Ianto Elen a Dai Shon Twmi
William John Jack a Ned Mari Jiny
Dai Lyw ar waelod y rhiw, a Rhys y Bear,
Mae e'n eitha byw
Dai Shon Crydd a Bessie First, na fachan â `thirst`
Wil Anti Kit a Bessie Camra Lisi'r Bont a Bili bach Sara
Ianto Blaine a Jack gwr Maggie, Freddie Shwt a Dai Mannie.
Dai Harri'r Joiners, y tenor "Gwych Sain" a Dan y Barber a'i goesau main
Wil y North sydd yn Gymro i'r bon, mae ei wraig o Lwynhendy a fo o Sir Fôn
Ned Mari Morgan a Griff y Crydd
John Abel, a Dan Pontypridd.
Dennis y Chemist, hen fachan gwirion
Dim yn y siop, o hyd yn y stesion
Dai Mawr a Padler Bach, enwau rhyfedd, howyr bach.
Mari'r Goder a Bryn bach y White
Davy John Nelson, hen fachan olreit
Glyn bach Ann a Frank y Red Cow
Y ddau 'n canu bas (both singing low)
Dai Swancs a John Fan acw
Dau enw smala, ond pert ofnadw
Ben y Nailor a Dic y Crân
Elwyn Powerhouse a Dai Penârn.
Wil y Paent a Jack Bara Jam
Enwau cymwys, i chi'n gwybod pam.
William John Pensteps a Freddie Twll
Efans y Broli a'r Hen Dwm o'r Pwll
Bogel Bach a Dai Hendy

Wil Cerrig Calch, hen fachan reit handi,
William Henry Booth a Dai Crwys
Dau enw da, a rheini ar bwys.
Oliver Chaplin a Sid Sand
Enwau rhyfedd ond yn swno'n grand.
Evans chocolates a Blew Bach
Heb angofio wrth gwrs fo Wil Bynea Fach
Jim Coconuts a Wil Mary.
Sdim enwau fel hyn i'w cael heddi.
Twm Sers a Liw Caws
Dau gymeriad hyfryd eu naws
Jac Brynffynnon a Wil Nellie
Hywel Rachel a Llew o'r Gelli
Jacob y Ship a Bowen y Pack
Oli'r Plough a Tomi Black
A dyma ddau enw a thipyn o dash
Sef - Pope John a Dai Backslash
Dai'r Genwen a John Broli
Peg Tŷ Front a Wil Twm Shoni
Wyn y chips a Jac y Llath
Dau gymeriad fu erioed eu math
Bili Twlpyn a Jac y Bwli
Ac mi allwn fynd mlan nes bore 'fory
Ond rwyf am derfynu gyda dau gyfaill clos-
Sef Raymond y Blode, a Mr Dai Tosh.

Bryn Davies

Bryn Davies Heol Hên.

Y Tabernacl, Eglwys y Bedyddwyr, Llwynhendy

Mae eglwys y Tabernacl wedi bod yn Llwynhendy ers 1895 ac yn dal i fod yn weithgar yn yr ardal. Mae'r festri wedi cael moderneiddio er mwyn gallu ei defnyddio yn ystod yr wythnos er budd y gymuned leol.

Yn ogystal ag oedfaon y Sul mae'na nifer o weithgareddau eraill yn cael ei cynnal.

Dyma rai ohonynt:

Tabernacle Baptist Chapel, Llwynhendy

Tabernacl Chapel has been in Llwynhendy since 1895, and is still active in the local community . The vestry has been modernised so it can be used during the week . Apart from the Sunday Services , there are a number of other activities held there.

Here are some of them .....

Clwb Sul

Cynhelir Clwb Sul ar gyfer plant 3 i 11 oed yn festri'r Tabernacl, Llwynhendy pob pnawn Sul yn ystod tymor yr ysgol. Mae'r plant yn cael cyfle i fwynhau amrywiaeth o weithgaredd au megis crefft, canu, gemau a thaflenni gwaith wedi eu seillio ar hanesion o'r Beibl.

Prynhawn o hwyl a sbri yng nghwmni Martyn Geraint, Medi 2008.

Sunday Club

This club is for children between the ages of 3 to 11 and is held in the vestry every Sunday afternoon during the school term . The children enjoy many activities such as craft, singing, games and work sheets which are based on stories from the Bible.

Clwb Haf y Plant

Ers 2004 mae'r Tabernacl wedi cynnal clwb plant llwyddiannus iawn am wythnos bob Haf. Mae yr ardal yn mwynhau chwarae gemau, cwblhau cwisiau, canu caneuon bywiog, gwaith crefft a chlywed storiau Beiblaidd wedi eu cyflwyno mewn dulliau cyffrous a gwreiddiol.

Children's Summer Club

Since 2004 Tabernacl held a very successful Summer Club for a week every summer. The children enjoy playing games, quizzes, singing, craft work and listening to stories from the Bible portrayed in original and exciting ways.

Plant y Clwb Sul yn dilyn Cyfarfod Y Pasg 2010 / The children of the Sunday Club following a special Easter Service 2010.

Siop Eunice y Painter

(Eunice the Painter's Shop)

Originally owned by Dan Richards, a prosperous painter and decorator, who sold it to Evan Williams who turned it into the village shop. His daughter took it over on his death and it became 'Siop Eunice y Painter'. The shop became the meeting place for all the women of Llwynhendy who congregated in the shop every evening for a good gossip that lasted until almost midnight on a good night!

Margaret Bonorelli, 2010

Ysgol Brynsierfel

This school, Ysgol Brynsierfel was officially opened on Thursday, 15th October, 1953. It was opened by the Right Honourable James Griffiths M.P.LL.D., and the ceremony was expertly presided over by the Alderman Douglas Hughes J.P., Chairman of Carmarthenshire Education Committee.

In the presence of a large number of members from the County Education Committee, members of the Local Education Committee, and the parents of the pupils, the ceremonial key was presented to Mr James Griffiths, by the County Architect Mr W. T. Lloyd and the Contractor Mr Sidney Jones, Llanelli.

Before opening the door Mr James Griffiths said that this was the second school that he had opened, the first being in Singapore and now this one in Llwynhendy. He felt it a great honour to be opening Brynsierfel Welsh School, and praised the choice of such an enchantingly pretty name for the school.

Rhan o gofnod Mr Ronald Thomas o'r Seremoni Agor.

Part of Mr Ronald Thomas' account of the Opening Ceremony.

Mr Ronald Thomas oedd y Prif Athro cyntaf Ysgol Brynsierfel.
Mr Ronald Thomas was the first Headmaster of Ysgol Brynsierfel.

Rhai o blant Ysgol Brynsierfel - 1968?
Some of the pupils of Brynsierfel School - 1968?

Aeth disgyblion a staff Ysgol Gymraeg Brynsierfel i fyny i weld sut roedd Cwmni Kier yn dod ymlaen gyda'r adeilad newydd ar 29.3.10 yn eu gwisgoedd Cymreig. Mae'r ysgol newydd sy'n costio 6.5 miliwn ac mi fydd yn barod ar gyfer y disgyblion ym Mis Medi 2011. Mae'r ysgol newydd yn cael ei adeiladu ar safle'r hen ysgol. Yn y llun mae 174 o blant yr ysgol, y Staff, y Pennaeth Mrs. Susan Bowen a Rheolwr y site Mr. Ewart Wilson.

Ysgol-yr-Ynys

This school was opened in 1950/51 as a feeder school for Llwynhendy School, to accommodate the large volume of children moving into the area. It was intended to remain open for ten years, but is in full use for education today in 2010.

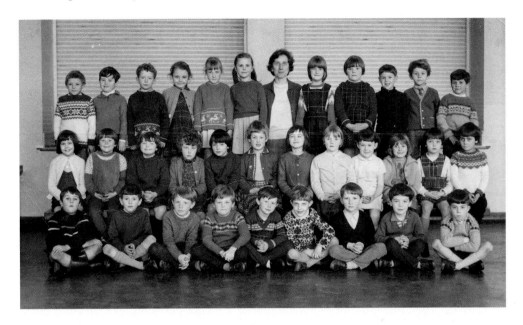

Ysgol yr Ynys
Teacher: Miss Joyce Thomas, Teacher's Assistant; Mrs Neilian Williams.

Jonah Yr Ynys, Myth or Miracle?

Jonah John was a young man when he came and settled in Llwynhendy. He was born in a cottage near Llanddowror. Young Jonah became a farmhand at a very early age, and after serving at various places, he married and settled down at the Ynys Farm, Llwynhendy.

Now Jonah was a familiar figure in the area, where he killed and dressed pigs. He was a well built character who wore a neckerchief and a flat cap over his unruly mass of hair. He was careless of his clothes, and besides being original in appearance, he was also original in character. He was a faithful and calciferous supporter of Soar Chapel, and when a proposal was make to install an organ in the Chapel he expressed his objection by compiling a hymn which began:

> "Nid yw sain gwefysau'r organ
> Ddim yn myn'd i glustiau Duw"
> ("The sound of the organ does not reach the ears of God")

He also objected to indoor baptising, that the rite of the Baptism should only take place in the river.

Around the 1870's there was a severe summer drought. Now it went on for months, and as there were no facilities for water in those days, all the fresh water came from ponds or water butts, which was collected off the roofs. The drought was so severe that the animals were dying. Then one moonlit evening Jonah or Ynys got down on his knees and made an impassioned plea to God for rain. The next morning the pond in front of the house was full of water, although it had not rained. Farmers from all over the area brought their animals to the little Ynys Farm to water. Jonah was a Saviour.

There is no explanation for a dried out pond being full of water, with no evidence of rainfall, but I can imagine the response to it in those religious days.

Jonah was the father to nine children and his legacy has been carried on through the game of rugby. Of the nine children came grand children. First was Dr Roy Thomas' father Gethin, one cap to Wales 1929, next was me, then my brother Len 1953-1955, then came Barry John and his brother Alan, then came Jonathan Davies, Barry John's sister Madora married Derek Quinnell and the Quinnell Dynasty came next.

Terry Davies 2010

Y Tywydd

Adroddiad Digri

Welsoch chi erioed shwd dywydd, gwedwch yn onest
Man'n ddigon i'ch hala chi i nido mas drwy'r ffenest.
Stecs fan hyn, a mwd fan draw
A phawb a'i scitshe yn dwlpin o faw,
Mae hyd yn nod y ffowls yn edrych yn sal
Yn ofni pob dydd i ddod mas o'i gwal,
Y cwn ar cathe, sydd lan hyd eu bagle
Ma nhw'n ofni ishte, o achos y cagle
`Stim ryfedd fod y ieir yn cadw shwd stwr
Os par hi fel hyn, bydd y wyau'n llawn dwr
A'r gwynt na pwy noswaith, Wel bobl dyna le
Rown yn credu fod popeth yn mynd o dre.
Rhwng fod Mari yn gwaeddi, a'r gwely yn crynu
A'r bapa yn schrechen wedi colli ei ddymu
Ffenestri yn clatshan a'r cwrtens yn hofran
A haner y shimle yn cwmpo i'r pentan,
Cafan yn cwmpo ar ben y churn lath
A slaten yn cwmpo ar ben y gath
Cwarel yn torri yn ffenest y gegin
A llun Lloyd George yn yfflon ar y landin
'Rown ni'n dechreu credu fod diwedd y byd
Ond trwy drugaredd wyf yma o hyd,
Pan death bore dranoeth fe welsom y damage
R'oedd drws y ty bach ar ben y garage,
A pen y twlc yng nghardd drws nesa
Ar moch yn screchen am y mwya,
Coeden anferth ar ben gat y clos
A'r ceiliog Rhode Island wedi torri ei gos,
Dwy'r tywydd yn siwto neb on wyed a pysgod,
Yn wir os na ddaw pethe yn well yn union
Mi fyddwn i gyd yn llawn o'r gwynegon
Rwyn terfynu yn awr, cyn daw rhagor o law
So long I chi nawr, cawn scwrs fach maes o law

Bryn Davies, Heol Hen

Parti'r Llwyn

Bu Parti'r Llwyn yn enwog, trwy Gymru gyfan yn y 50au a'r 60au. Roedd y parti yn hanu o Llwynhendy ac yn cynnwys:- Dilys Evans, Mary V. Evans, ac Alfryn Evans, Geirwyn Davies, Brin Davies, David H. Evans a Nanci Thomas. Mr Vic Thomas oedd arweinydd y parti canu a chynhaliwyd ymarferion i'w cyngherddau yn Ffermdy Heol Hen, Llwynhendy. Teithiodd y parti ledled Cymru, i gynnal Nosweithiau Llawen a fe wnaeth y parti berfformio i Gymdeithas Cymru Llundain ar sawl achlysur. Aelodau o'r parti oedd yn cynhyrchu deunydd gwreiddiol i'w caneuon a'u sgetsis. Recordiwyd llawer o rhaglenni gan Parti'r Llwyn i B.B.C. Radio Cymru yn enwedig y rhaglen 'Dewch am dro' gydag Alun Williams.

Parti'r Llwyn were well known throughout Wales in the 1950's and 60's. The concert party from Llwynhendy, consisted of :- Dilys Evans, Mary V. Evans, Alfryn Evans, Geirwyn Davies, Brin Davies, David H. Evans and Vic & Nansi Thomas. Mr Vic Thomas was the party's leader and rehearsals for concerts were held at Heol Hen Farmhouse, Llwynhendy. The party held 'Nosweithiau Llawen' in many areas of Wales and performed at the London Welsh Club on many occasions. Members of Parti'r Llwyn composed their own music and produced original scripts for sketches. Many programmes were recorded by the party for B.B.C. Radio Wales.

Rhian Lewis (gynt/nee Evans)

Pati'r Llwyn - Eisteddfod Abergwain (Fishguard)
Left to right: Vic Thomas, Mary V. Evans, Nansi Thomas, Dilys Evans, Geirwyn Davies, Bryn Davies, ac Alfryn Evans.

'Parti'r Llwyn' of Llwynhendy, who gave an evening's entertainment (Noson Lawen) at London Welsh Club, Grey's Inn Road . Their leader Mr Vic Thomas is second right.

Erw Las

We now leave Heol Hen Farm, passing where Tir Einon once stood, and return to the bottom of Parc Gitto and Llwyn Hall and continuing along Erw-las, heading to the Bridges, `Y Bontydd` a favourite walk for the villagers of Bynea and Llwynhendy with their prams or a Sunday evening stroll after Chapel.

History and Recollections of Parc Einon Farm

The first mention of Parc Einon was in an old document dated 1808, but it is not clear whether it was a conveyance of land only, or whether a building was in existence at that time. However James Hopkin 1788 1877, who's nick name was Shams o'r Lan, lived at Parc Einon from 1841 with his first wife Elizabeth. (see census 1841). And in 1852 the farm was again leased by William Chambers to James Hopkin. (See James Hopkin's Will)

When Elizabeth died, James married his housekeeper Ann Lewis, who was 40 years younger than him. They had six children. Their son David Hopkins lived at Parc Einon with his first wife Catherine (Daughter of Titus and Margaret Jones of the Butcher's Arms Cwmfelin, and later with his second wife Mary in the 1880's and 90's).

David and Mary's daughter Annie Jane (born 1890) had many memories of her childhood which she recalled from time to time. These were, of walking home along a narrow country Jane in the dark, and being afraid of the overhanging trees, of the smell of salted bacon hanging on a meat hook in an outhouse and of running across three fields to meet her father coming home from the coal mine. He would hoist her up on his shoulders and carry her home. She also remembered her father standing in front of the fire dressed in his Sunday his frockcoat ready for chapel, and she watched him tend livestock and mend fences. She recalled seeing him struggle to do this work as he had a hacking cough. No time to appreciate the beautiful view or the peace of the countryside. Life was hard, and when Annie was six years old, her father died.

Dr. E. Hector Beynon Hopkins former Medical Officer of Health for Llanelli and great grandson of James Hopkin, recollected that;

> "Parc Einon Farm was a stone built cottage with one or two small fields and 4 or 5 acres of grazing rights of the marsh. It had two rooms downstairs and two rooms upstairs. In the 1930s under the direction of father (Revd. J. H. Beynon Hopkins) John, my brother and I removed the thatch on the cottage. Beynon's nephew David Emlyn Hopkins replaced the thatch with galvanised zinc sheeting."

The photograph on the next page (reproduced with permission from Mr. Samuel) shows the farm in the 1960's/70's when it was owned by the Samuel family.

On 4th March 1985 Parc Einon farm was acquired by the Borough Council in connection with the Wildlife and Wetlands Trust. It was demolished, and all that remains is the small garden, which can be viewed at the Wildlife and Wetlands Centre at Penclacwydd.

The tangible evidence of past generations in this cottage are gone for ever. Only the sighing of the wind in the reeds mourn its passing.

> "Every hamlet, town and parish, every mountain, river and valley, every cottage and mansion has a history ... it is true in our little corner of the county we cannot boast of huge Norman castles or gorgeous palaces, but we have the silent chronicles of the peaceful worker and the labourers ..."

Quotation by Mr. James Morgan Jones (son of the Butcher's Arms) and headmaster of Five Roads School in an article to The Star Newspaper 1939, shortly before his death.

Marion Martin 2010

Penclacwydd

The several hundred hectares of low lying land surrounding the centre was formerly saltmarsh around 200 years ago. This area - Morfa Mawr - The Great Saltmarsh (or Llanelly Marsh as it was also called) was reclaimed with the construction of the Great Embankment or bulwark of the Enclosure Award 1807 (Carmarthenshire's first Enclosure Act) which produced approximately 245 hectares of land for development alone.

In 1983, and at the request of the Llanelli Borough Council, the then Wildfowl Trust produced a study of the potential for a WWT Centre which would form part of the Council's tourism strategy. In all three sites were identified by the Council for the development of a WWT Centre – two near Kidwelly at the mouth of the estuary and the current site aptly named Penclacwydd (translated means Head of the Gander/Goose) one of the seven farms which served the existing holding.

Work began on creating the centre in December 1985. The initial work on the ground was carried out by a local work force, part of the then Manpower Services Commission's 'Community Programme Scheme' This Scheme finished in February 1989, over two years before the Centre opened. By then some full time and contracted staff had been taken on by WWT to continue and complete the development which was opened to the Public on April 17th 1991 by Sir David Attenborough.

The original 125 year leasehold of approximately 135ha then comprised of two main areas;

The Grounds – an area of approximately 19ha landscaped grounds, ponds and pathways which was developed for the Collection the industrial past it used to literally run red due to iron oxide and pollutants that used to be flushed into it - thankfully this is no longer the case!

Area. The water that feeds into the pens here is pumped up from the Afon Goch (translated means Red River) where it eventually returns.

In 1998 work started on the creation of the Millennium Wetlands – an 80ha development and extension of WWT's holding to 196ha in total.

The Millennium Wetlands was opened by Rolf Harris in July 2000 and has, by its design, turned the clock back 200 years by restoring the land back to wetland (as a freshwater version).

In 2003 the reserve entered into the Tir Gofal Scheme. Tir Gofal is a relatively new all Wales agri-environmental scheme delivered on behalf of the National Assembly by the Countryside Council for Wales in partnership with the Farming & Rural Conservation Agency. Additional management under the scheme includes grazing by cattle and horses in the Millennium Wetland and the reintroduction of cattle on the saltmarsh and surrounding fields.

We would like to thank Mr John Saunders for putting together the account on Penclacwydd.

Penelacwydd

Yr alarch balch yn ei bali
Ar hwyaid yn nofio'n ddi-stŵr,
Y glaw o'r cymylau'n poeri
Ac ysgrifen y gwynt ar y dŵr.

Y fflamingo hirgoes yn sefyll
Fel hen filwr yn gwarchod ei stad,
Mewn lifrai rhuddgoch urddasol
Nawr ymhell o sŵn y gad.

Wynne H. Jones

Wynne Jones, Llwynhendy.

The Goal Posts (Berwick Roundabout)

Dedicating the old Stradey Park rugby ground goalposts (home of the Scarlets, Llanelli).
Many a goal has been kicked over these! Photographed Rev. Eldon Phillips, Terry Davies
and Derek Quinnell, taken on Boxing Day, 2009.

May the goalposts be a feature of Bynea and Llwynhendy, situated on the eastern gateway of the A484, as part of the Rugby Heritage Trail. It is there to attract worldwide visitors and also serves a dual purpose, to remind all Swansea supporters of their past disappointments when visiting old Stradey Park.

We now leave the Berwick roundabout, the new home for the famous goalposts, continuing to the end of the old favourite walk 'Y Bontydd' (the Bridges) towards Berwick Road, passing Techon Fach and Berwick farm and thus, we return back to the village of Bynea.

We have come to the end of our journey through the villages of Bynea and Llwynhendy. Looking back on the days and times of such a variety of historical interests, a wealth of culture and talent with surrounding natural beauty.

May your walk through these villages prove to you that village life is not dead, and that you will contribute to its prosperity in the coming years.

Part Five
Village Tales and Memoirs

Loughor River

When you cross the Loughor Bridge from the Glamorgan side imagine what you would have seen 2000 year ago. The Loughor Estuary would have been the largest sea port outside Rome and as it was the last port of call for Roman Ships it would have been quite busy, being the final loading place before setting sail to Rome.

The Romans mined the area extensively using Iron Ore and mining Coal to give them the necessary ingredients to produce steel weaponry in the Llandybie area. There is evidence of large limestone excavation in this search for precious metals - Gold, Silver and Tin which could be transported back to Rome. There would be boat building and fishing all along the Gower and Penclawdd fronts. It is said that two fishing villages have been taken over by the sea, as was the old island of Machynys. There is an old Escape Tunnel running from the old church in Loughor across the river to the old church in Pontarddulais (which has been removed to St Fagans in Cardiff). My father told me that there had been a preliminary exploration roughly about half way under the river where they found rusty swords and old helmets before the tunnel collapsed.

Nicknames

When they were employing labour for the Glynea Colliery in the early part of the 1900's, when coal became King again, the colliery had to look further afield for labour.

Of course, the names were limited to David or William etc., as there were so many similar names it was essential then to add a nickname to the initial name. A worker had arrived from another village and the foreman asked his name, he replied with the popular name of 'Dai', so the foreman said "You will be known with another name", so the man said "I hope you will name me something substantial!" so the foreman named him and for the rest of his life, he was known as 'Dai Substantial!'

Cabin Humour

Every works had 'little cabins' for the men to eat their meals. These became places for conversations the latest jokes and gossip. They were also places for 'Bragging Rights' where there would be challenges to the most outlandish made up stories. In this crowd there were serial liars who would brag about the most extreme challenges.

One story was from John the Ashes, who stood up and said, "Last year I went over the Niagara Falls in a barrel". There was a hushed silence and then John Abel's retort came like a rapier thrust. "Yes John he said, I saw you, I was there!"

W. J. Morris Coal Merchant

William John Morris was a coal agent for several mines, and during the First World War, the demand for the best steam coal was great. All our Naval ships relied on the steam coal, and as the Llanelli Coal was more gaseous, and volatile than other British coal, it became of huge importance to the Royal Navy, as its volatility gave our fleet to 2 knots greater speed over the German fleet. William John commissioned ships to sail to Malta with West Wales coal, Malta being the storage area for coal for the whole of the Mediterranean. It meant that our ships controlled that strategic area of sea. This was important, as the German army then had to receive all their supplies by land.

He was very fortunate not to lose any ships as this would have meant certain bankruptcy. There would be anxious moments until the ship arrived in Malta before the news of its arrival would reach Bynea.

W. J. was a good benefactor to the village paying a lot of the material costs for the building of the 1932 hall. He then donated a New Hall at the Genwen site to be used for concerts and plays, but the village never made proper use of it, as with the advent of radio and television people started to stay home rather than support the Hall. He quietly donated to the Chapel also, not seeking any recognition for his kindness.

Although he was the first village entrepreneur, he never forgot his roots in the welfare of his village.

The Ghost of Bynea

Should you travel through the village around 7a.m. you would have been confronted with the terrifying spectre of Phil the Ghost. This was Phil Richards who worked as the Baker in the Bake house. He would have been covered from head to toe with white flour and to see him in the half light would send shivers down your spine.

Bakers always worked at night and Phil would walk home the same time as the village men were going to work.

Blackout Time

Another character, Arthur Rees, a local farmer's son had a passion for donning a white sheet and pretending to be a ghostly figure. One evening he accosted David Eynon, Willie Walters and Jack Thomas the Butcher on their way home from the Red Cow Inn, who were a little worse for wear. As they were crossing the old Railway bridge which was humped back and very narrow, Arthur appeared in his white gown 'who-whooing'. David Eynon took one look at him and promptly struck him a blow which transported Arthur over the bridge wall to end up flattened on the railway below. There were sounds of great hilarity when they saw this severely limping ghost disappearing in the dark.

A Bachelor's Haven

Just after The Second World War a number of the village girls had married outsiders, men from other areas, some had married Englishmen, who had been based with the RAF at Pencoed Works, who had been billeted with families around the village. Some of the girls became GI Brides, and moved to America.

One notable lady was Muriel Gunn's mother who kept the Sweet Shop. Muriel, having become a widow has now returned to live with her brother in Llangennech.

The death of young girls may also have been the reason, for there were so many bachelors, young men of eligible age. A number of young men returned from the War and had simply settled into the old way of life.

The Vaughan's, the Hopkins, the Jones', of Saron Road. The Davies Family were to name just a few in all. There seemed to be more than fifty young men without a partner, this may have been responsible for the decline in the number of children attending the village school. In the 1930's there were 290 children in the school, in the 1950's there were only 140 children on the register, 60 years later the school has only around 100 pupils.

Black Market in the Blackout

Dewi Thomas told me the story of his father's exploits during the war time meat Black Market.

There was a small butchers shop in Hendre Road owned by the 'Parchedig' (The Reverend) David John Jones, Minister of Capel Bwlch Llan Morlais.

Every Sunday morning while he was preaching to his flock, a sheep or a pig would be slaughtered and deposited in a large fridge at the back of the shop, as being the day of the Sabbath there would be no prying eyes. On the Sunday night the meat would be placed in the back of Jack's car and taken to be sold in Llandeilo. During that time of night as well as the blackout there was always a chance they would be stopped by the police or the Home Guard, but with the Minister sitting in the front seat there was always a free passage, and an apology to the Minister who revealed his best dog collar, for stopping the car.

Another episode when they lived in the Bwlch Farm:

Jack had slaughtered a pig in the morning and then he had a tip off, that the police were on the way to search the farm. The children however failed to go to bed early as the pig was hidden in their bed 'probably snorting away!'

Trolley Buses

The fare for a return to Llanelli was 2 pence old money. They were run on electricity with a turning point by the St David's Tin works (Loughor Bridge), Yspitty.

It was 1936, and I was 4 years of age. My first memory of the trolleys were seeing them lit up for the Coronation, they had a crown lit up by small bulbs on the front, with more bulbs running down the top of the trolley to the back. The same crown would be at the back.

I remember the bonfire on the Glynea Tip of railway sleepers, crisscrossed on top of one another with great sparks rising to the sky, with the whole village gathering these to celebrate the Coronation.

Back to the trolley, it was a very effective means of travel as it was now possible to find work further afield, as well as to do shopping other than the village. It was the means of getting to the town cinemas and to see Llanelli play at the Stradey Park.

The weekend (Saturday) trip to Llanelli would include faggots and peas in the market, where you were given a bowl and a spoon and you waited your turn to be served from a large copper pan. You would then sit on long wooden tables and benches under an awning of canvas to enjoy your hot meal.

Then it was a choice of several cinemas, the Odeon, the Regal, the Hippodrome (Haggers), the Llanelli Cinema, the Palace and a small cinema in New Dock Road.

The cost of this extravaganza, faggots and peas 3 pence, trolley return 2 pence, cinema 9 pence, Maggie's fish and chips and a bottle of Tizer pop 6 pence. Grand Total 20 pence, 4 short of two shillings.

Bynea School Pupils 290

What I remember most of the school days was second hand me down clothes and in my case, third hand. Being the third boy in a family of six children it was short trousers until you were thirteen and your sweaters, (or Jerseys as they were called then), would be made of recycled wool from previous jumpers. My mother made me a most impressive Fair Isle sweater once with wool recycled from four garments, which was much admired.

From the early days in school there were coal fires in the winter and oak block flooring and half glassed doors, so that the headmaster could see into the classroom without entering. During the War all the windows were covered with strips of paper to stop them splintering, should any bombs blow them in. We used to keep the gas masks close to us at all times and when the air raid siren went we were allocated houses close to the school where we could go for shelter.

My mother insisted that all of us, Roy, Len, Marina and I should stay together as she couldn't bear for one to be lost-she would rather lose us all.

Hetty Rees was our 'safe house'. We would all run to Berwick Road and then shelter under Hetty's table. We would then be supplied with ready made sandwiches and cakes to be eaten under the table. The siren would always go in the early afternoon weather permitting, as if it was cloudy the German planes couldn't locate where to drop their bombs. We all prayed for good weather so that the Air Raid siren would sound so that we could go to Hetty Rees for refreshments.

The teachers at Bynea School in those days were:

Mr Isaac Thomas Headmaster; Mr Albert Rees; Miss Thomas; Miss Bowser (Infants Headmistress); Mr Bryn Jones Tenor, as well as 290 children.

Excursions

School holidays coincided with the chapel trip to Porthcawl by train. When the train arrived at Bynea Station it would be reminiscent of the Indian trains with every child on board leaning out of the windows waving like mad. The train was jam packed after stopping at Llangennech and Pontardulais. Everyone had packed meals to feed the children, which would be eaten on the beach near the Fair in Porthcawl. The miners from the Valleys would be there in strength and Porthcawl was full to the brim. After a hectic day with donkey rides and games the journey to Bynea was peaceful with most of the children fast asleep.

Rowntrees Chocolate Factory Bristol

The most forward looking trip for the older children was the train trip which took over 2 hours to get there. We were then taken around the factory, which ended in a large shop with everyone being given a chocolate bar as a gift. Perhaps the best part of this trip was the train journey as we were only allowed into a small area of the factory. The old adage seems apt here as 'its better to travel than to arrive!!'

Bynea Steel Works

One class was allowed to visit the Steelworks at a time, and I will always remember the noise and the heat, with the gantries moving back and fore swinging ladles full of moulten metal and the flames coming out of the furnaces, but the best part for me was the Blacksmith room where Jabez Thomas was King. We were fascinated by him beating a steel rod with such speed, it would glow red hot.

Hair Cuts for Boys , Ringlets for Girls

As there were large families in the village, when it came to cutting the children's hair it was 'Do it yourself' barbering. With the poorer families it was a case of fitting a basin over their heads and simply cutting around the basin rim, consequently most of the boys looked like an early style of the Beatles: sometimes the basin would slip and the boy would look lop sided until his next hair cut.

The girls hair were in Ringlets and every evening before going to bed strips of cloth were platted into twirls which were called skilps or piglets. To be seen with these by boys outside the family the girls would be horrified and they would disappear up to their beds shrieking in embarrassment.

Ailments

Nearly every child in the village would have the Croup which was a nasty cough which went on for ever and then you would be submitted to the extreme torture of the hot goose grease poultice, plastered on your chest and you would go round for days with your nostrils flared from this sickening smell. If you were not cured you were then submitted to the second torture and you were taken down to Llanelli Station and taken on the train to Swansea. In between stations was Cocket tunnel. Once the train had entered the tunnel the window was lowered and your head was stuffed out to breath the steam. I still remember being `spit washed` with about 30 other children by the mothers and we all looked as if we had measles, only the spots were black smut

RAF Pencoed Works

During the War the works became an aeroplane recycling plant, where crashed and damaged air planes were transported from all over the country to be cannibalised for reusable parts to be used for spares for the existing fleet of planes.

There were Spitfires and Hurricanes and Lockhead Lightnings with lightweight bodies made out of ply wood so that they could boost their speed to `out run` the German planes. The Lockhead Lightening was usually used for reconnaissance flights or photographing bomb damage of German targets.

What a playground for us children. We would sit in the cockpits of these planes and dream of shooting down the Luftwaffe planes. We would then take a piece of the Perspex wind screen and make rings for our fingers out of them they became precious mementos as we had never seen Perspex before.

Winter Meals

Cawl with marrow bone from the butcher.
Home made faggots and peas.
Ham and pea soup.
Tripe and onions.
Bartering items would be eggs for margarine.
Dried milk and Canadian Chocolate powder.

Every Sunday night I went down to Glynea Terrace where the Pelosi's lived, they were Italians and kept a cafe in Swansea. I would take down 1 dozen eggs, I would knock the door and when the door was opened this coffee smell would waft out. Now no one else drunk coffee in the village, so it was a strange smell, not a word was said, the eggs were passed over, the door was shut. I would stand there in the blackout for 5 minutes. Then, the door would open and two half pound bars of margarine would be given to me. The door would shut and not a word had been spoken.

Meals

The meals were varied and nutritious. My mother baked every day, around 10 loaves a week. The best bread I ever tasted. There would be cockles, lava bread, bacon and egg on Saturdays. Sunday lunch would be a brisket of beef cooked for hours to soften it. Monday, left overs, Tuesday was succulent sticky rabbit, cooked in a roaster pan with liver and onions. Wednesday a well cooked heart, Thursday egg and chips and Friday was either liver an onions or fish caught in the estuary. There would be apple tart and custard for afters or a jam sponge, utility tart which was pastry jam and custard on top, but my favourite was bread and butter pudding made out of 2 stale loaves of bread (half price). On special occasions there would be chicken.

During the War we kept chickens at the top of the garden and sometimes it was necessary to kill one to make a meal. As all the chickens had names, my father would always ruin the meal by commenting how tasty Maisy or Daisy would be.

There was a thriving Black Market in the village where the bartering system worked very well. Certain items like eggs could be exchanged for another produce. A pig would be killed, and the meat would be exchanged for butter or sugar.

It was strange however, whenever a pig was killed it had to be done secretly as it was against the law to keep unregistered animals. The day of the execution would be known by everyone as the pig used to squeal so loudly everyone for miles could hear it. The village policeman would always have a day off and would be somewhere else, but the next day he would call for his share of the pig.

Play Grounds

The two collieries in the village were the Genwen and the Glynea pits (Pwll Y Bont), with the Glynea Tip the meeting place for all the village children in the winter because it became the San Moritz of Bynea, and with 6 inches of snow on the ground it became a Slalem Run with three or four children riding on a make shift sledge, an old tin sheet turned up at the front and a hair raising run down the steepest side of the old tip. There was no means of stopping and the brake would be the thick hedge at the very bottom. The crash would throw everyone off and you would always end up full of scrapes and the odd limp.

There were still old steam tanks lying near the old pit entrance and during the War we would pretend they were submarines and we would be sinking the German fleet on a regular basis. Near Berwick Farm 500 yards from the Glynea Pit was the Pit Air duct and escape hole for the colliery, it was around 80 yards deep which was the lowest working seam, and it had an iron ladder all the way down as an escape hatch, should there be an explosion in the mine.

It was also the means of bringing fresh air to the miners when the mine closed, this air hole was capped but part of the concrete had dislodged where you could drop a stone into the water to the bottom. In the summer you would count to 23 but in the winter the water table would rise and you would only count to 7 or 8 depending on the rainfall.

Genwen Colliery and Quarry

The Genwen area was different it had trees and ferns growing on it and was ideal Cowboy and Indian country, you could hide in the vegetation and ambush the stage coach, rob a bank and shoot all the poor Indians all in one go. The place was alive with wild life and a run through the heather would scatter rabbits galore with the odd snake about 4 feet long.

At one time the area had been home to about 7 railway coaches dotted around about 2 acres of land. These were sold by railway companies and delivered to Llangennech Railway Station then loaded on to a flat cart and then drawn by 6 horses. They were transported up the steep gradient from Llangennech up to the Bryn, and then down to Bynea, where they were rolled off the cart by wooden rollers on to a flat area. The back section would then be cut to make way for a stone chimney to supply a cooking area.

Some of the people bought 2 carriages which were bolted together making living quarters out of one side and bedrooms in the other. There are some people still living who resided in these, there were the Millers, the Coopers, the Beechams, David Thomas, and the Prestons.

They were living there with no electricity, or water. All the water had to be carried from the communal water tap which was sited on the wall next to Maggie Jones' Chip Shop. The depression in the wall where the tap was is still visible today.

The last double carriage was removed from Pendderi 2 years ago (Ewart Thomas Red Cow) by the Llanelli Railway Society and are currently stored in Cynheidre, where they will be refurbished as museum pieces. The date on both carriages, which was oak built was 1882.

Sunday School

All the children went to Sunday School. You were dressed up and went to Saron Chapel, which is now Saron Hall. I suppose it gave your parents time to relax after Sunday lunch away from the chore of looking after the family. It was quite pleasant, we were taught the scripture stories and we sang a few songs mainly in Welsh. On occasions we would go over to the Gospel Hall in Station Road as they would have nice children's parties.

Then, Sunday evenings, six clock Soar Chapel to fidget on the hard seats for an hour and a half.

Washing Days

Monday was washing day and the village fluttered with blowing clothes. Every washing line in the village would be 40 yards long, 3 line posts, to accommodate the large wash. Everyone had the old scrubber and wringer, and every child had stuck his or her fingers into the wringer, it seemed to mesmerise every child.

If there was no school we would meet under the old archway in the middle of Cwmfelin Row. The archway being the access of back entrance to the row of 30 houses. If there was a good drying wind blowing I would stand in the middle of 30 rows of washing with the bed sheets flapping like ship sails. I would close my eyes and I would be transported on to Nelson's Flagship giving chase to the French Fleet. What glorious Mondays.

It was easily recognisable what line belonged to what family. One lady in the row was by far the largest woman in the village. Her two pairs of bloomers in red made the biggest statement of all, like two great windsocks fully inflated blowing majestically in the wind. You could identify who lived in the house by the washing nappies and children's clothes meant the younger parents Long Johns were for the older men, all blowing with sagging bottoms to them. The young women were more discreet drying underwear by the fire.

To have a clean wash on the line was a source of great pride to behold. The not too clean clothes - they were always talked about as having, in the words of my mother pug washing . They were not classed on the same level as the spotless washers.

Christmas Time

When the pigs head with an orange stuck in its mouth appeared in Jack the Butcher's window we knew Christmas had arrived and all the children would gather round the window to admire the orange. As it was war time, fruit was very scarce, there would be some apples and some pears which had survived until Christmas being carefully wrapped in newspaper and kept in a cardboard box in a dark place. Exotic fruits such as bananas and pineapples were non-existent and we didn't see these until well after the War had ended.

Christmas stockings were hung on the bed post and there was always a rush to get the longest stocking. These normally would be stockings worn with Wellingtons. What excitement when you woke early and the stocking was full, there would be an apple, new socks, nuts and the ever present packet of sticky dates. There were never any toys, instead there would be some clothes, always too large for you, so that you would grow into them.

All the children would be up and about early looking with envy at some of the wealthier families' presents. Christmas Eve all the chickens to be cooked would be carried over to the Bake house for Willie Perks to cook in the large Dutch oven. The glorious smells emanating from the Bake house captured you and we all lingered enjoying the smells of Christmas cooking.

Christmas afternoon we spent listening to the King's Speech on the radio and Billy Cotton's `Wakey Wakey` show.

Terry Davies

The Bynea Cycling Club

The date is Thursday March 25th 1937, and you open 'The Llanelly Mercury' and there in the 'Llwynhendy & Bynea District News' is an invitation to all those who are interested in cycling to attend a meeting, with the hope of forming a club. The meeting is to be held in the Welfare Pavilion Bynea on the following Monday (Easter Monday) March 29th 1937, at 11a.m. and the invitation is from W. E. Wheeler.

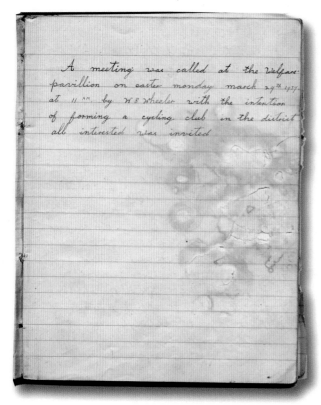

A meeting was called at the welfare pavillion on easter monday march 29th 1937 at 11 AM by W.S wheeler with the intention of forming a cycling club in the district all interested was invited

Twenty local boys turned up at the meeting that Monday morning, and it was proposed by Mr Jack Richards, that the club should be formed, this was seconded by Mr Jack Grove, and it was carried.

Jack Grove then proposed that it should be known as the 'Bynea Cycling Club'.

We are informed from the minutes book of that meeting, not only that it was decided to form a club, but they immediately elected officials as follows;

Dr B. D. Hughes - President
Jack Grove - Hon. Chairman
Cyril Edwards - Hon. Treasurer
W. E. Wheeler - Hon. Secretary

It was also proposed that the Club, if accepted, should be affiliated to the National Cyclist Union.

The annual fee for membership to the club was proposed as 3/6 (17½p in todays money), which included the N.C.U. fee (National Cycling Union), which would be paid on the 1st January of each year.

After discussion it was decided that their headquarters (if approved by the Welfare Committee) should be the Welfare Pavilion.

The committee for 1937/38 was also decided on that morning. A. Bibby proposed that membership should be open to both sexes, and this was seconded by Jack Grove and carried through. They started with only 20 members, that morning, but in their first year the membership rose from 20 to 30 members, leading eventually to a 100 members, and of those 100, 30-40 were Bynea boys.

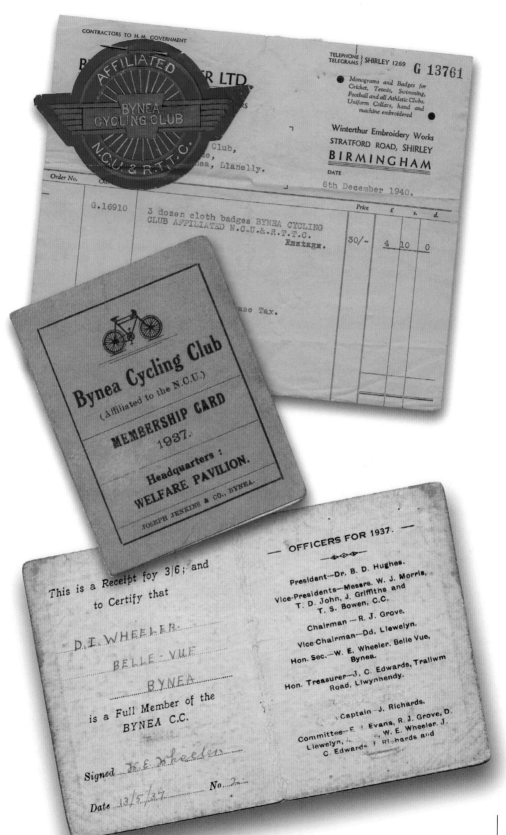

CONTRACTORS TO H.M. GOVERNMENT

B......... ......R LTD.

TELEPHONE } SHIRLEY 1269
TELEGRAMS } **G 13761**

● Monograms and Badges for
Cricket, Tennis, Swimming,
Football and all Athletic Clubs.
Uniform Collars, hand and
machine embroidered

Winterthur Embroidery Works
STRATFORD ROAD, SHIRLEY
BIRMINGHAM

DATE

6th December 1940.

.... Club,
.... ne,
.... nea, Llanelly.

Order No.

			Price	£	s.	d.
G.16910	3 dozen cloth badges BYNEA CYCLING CLUB AFFILIATED N.C.U.&.R.T.T.C. Xxxxxxx.		30/-	4	10	0

......ase Tax.

AFFILIATED
**BYNEA
CYCLING CLUB**
N.C.U. & R.T.T.C.

Bynea Cycling Club
(Affiliated to the N.C.U.)
MEMBERSHIP CARD
1937.

Headquarters :
WELFARE PAVILION.

JOSEPH JENKINS & CO., BYNEA.

This is a Receipt foy 3/6; and
to Certify that

D.T. WHEELER

BELLE-VUE

BYNEA

is a Full Member of the
BYNEA C.C.

Signed W.E Wheeler

Date 13/5/37   No. 2

— OFFICERS FOR 1937.

President—Dr. B. D. Hughes.

Vice-Presidents—Messrs. W. J. Morris,
T. D. John, J. Griffiths and
T. S. Bowen, C.C.

Chairman — R. J. Grove.

Vice-Chairman—Dd. Llewelyn.

Hon. Sec.—W. E. Wheeler, Belle Vue,
Bynea.

Hon. Treasurer—J. C. Edwards, Trallwm
Road, Llwynhendy.

Captain — J. Richards.

Committee—F. I Evans, R. J. Grove, D.
Llewelyn, ..., W. E. Wheeler, J.
C. Edwards ? Richards and

Bynea Cycling club leaving for Carreg Cennen castle.

In 1938 as their contribution to 'National Fitness Week', the club organised a run to cater for as many men cyclist in the area at the time. Twenty riders set off for Carreg Cennen Castle via Paxtons Tower. Tea was arranged at The Trapp Inn, which was very rare in those years.

So it was, that the Bynea Cycling Club had been formed and it is still in existence today 73 years later. In the early days the Club held runs mostly on Saturdays and Sundays, and weekend runs at Easter and Whitsun. The Saturday runs were generally round trips of 50 miles, and always started from the Welfare ground, while the Sunday runs always started from the town Hall in Llanelli, and were longer. Often they would go to places like Builth Wells or Brecon, a round trip of 100 miles.

Unfortunately for the Club, just as they were becoming well known and successful in the cycling world the War intervened, but they were determined to carry on in spite of the fact that many of their members went to the Forces. They continued to keep going throughout the War years, but many changes had to be made as one by one the officials, as well as the members left for the Forces. By November 1942 they had lost Islwyn as well as his brother Willie, their General Secretary. He was the 13th member of the Club to be called up.

To keep the interest going in the early years of the War they decided in January 1941 to set up a challenge cycling match on rollers between Stan Bates of the Grovesend, Welfare Cycling Club and D.I. Wheeler of Bynea, and was held in the Bynea Recreation Club - it was won by the local champion but Bates did not give up and throughout January and into March the challenge continued in different venues. Eventually the match was decided over 3 events at ¼, ½, and 1 mile events. Wheeler won by 2 events to 1.

As the War continued and the members were called up, those left behind were determined to keep the Club going, so it was decided to allow younger members of the community to join the club.

When the men returned after the War, they continued where they had left off and the Cycling Club went from strength to strength.

Membership has fluctuated over the years reaching a peak of 150 in 1951 and then declined gradually to an all time low of 20 in 1964. Since then however it has risen steadily to the present level of 90+.

The club has been very fortunate in the quality of its officials over the years with W.J. Jenkins and his wife Anne overseeing the 1930's/40 who both worked tirelessly on behalf of the club. In 1951, W. Graham John became secretary and was to stay until 1971 bringing efficiency and providing information to club members which opened up new cycling activities such as Youth hostelling and touring holidays.

Following Graham the club found a real diamond in Mrs Betty Owen who emulated her predecessors efficiency and dedication for 22 years until resigning in 1993.

The clubs first long serving treasurer was D. Arthur Jones who for 20 years 1964-1966 controlled the club finances with meticulous attention to detail down to the last half penny.

Following on from Arthur, another person in the form of Tom Samuel took over the financial reins and did so for 25 years 1973-1998.

Other who have given valuable service to the club in numerous and various positions are Tudor Thomas (the present treasurer) Phill Jones, Alan Owen, and John Bevan (chairman)

In 1976 following long term endeavour the club squired their own home when on October 9th 1976 they officially opened their own club room at Heol y Bwlch Bynea.

ERCURY, THURSDAY, OCTOI

Llwynhendy & District

CYCLIST BROTHERS IN ITALY

News has reached home of the meeting of Willie and Islwyn, sons of Mr. William Wheeler and the late Mrs. Wheeler, of 3, Belle Vue, Bynea, in Italy. Willie, who is serving with the

Mr. Islwyn Wheeler.

R.A., has been with the 5th Army from the start of their fighting in Italy. Islwyn, who is in the R.E., is attached to a Port Operating Co. and saw service in North Africa previous to his removal to Italy. One day a hospital ship pulled in the port where Islwyn was engaged, and on reaching the quayside he heard his name being called. Still unaware of his brother's presence, he dashed to the gangway, only to meet Willie, who was on board being evacuated to an Italian hospital. It is gratifying to note that he has since been discharged from hospital and is

Mr. Willie Wheeler.

convalescent. Previou

119

A lot of hard work by members, digging out, laying foundations and erecting the building, overseen by builder and club member Alan Owen culminated in a successful conclusion. During the club room managing director of Bynea based Thyssen G.B. Mr Richard Englert was a great source of help in providing the club with the use of his organisations legal and administrative department, but most important with his generosity in providing the land for the club.

The club has been an asset and is ideally located with a very short distance of the cycle path to the west.

On the competitive side the club has enjoyed great success at many types of racing. At massed start road racing the club has had 5 rides competing for Wales. Alan Owen, Tudor Thomas, Martin Harsant, Phill Jones and John Holt. At the time trailing? Was the main club racing activity, and the club has won numerous team awards at West Wales and National level.

Welsh Champions from the club are Tudor Thomas, Nigel Lewis, John Holt, and Chris Bates, and Tudor Malcolm Lucus. Nigel, John, and Chris have been crowned welsh Best all-rounders Champions in the competition involving rides at 50-100 miles in 12 hours, the ultimate time trailing achievement.

Thousands of cyclists have been involved in the club over the past 70 years, and the strength of the club at present is looking well for the future, during which thousands more will enjoy cycling with the club in a location which is ideal for cycling when you leave the few towns in the area, and enjoy the Gower Coast, Gwendraeth Valleys, Towy Valley, and Llwchwr river area.

In the last 2 years there has been resurgence of activity in club runs, rides of a social, leisurely nature, with café stops, brought about as a result of the enthusiasm of rejoined members Paul Rees who has succeeded where others have failed in rebuilding participation in the activity which has been dormant for many years.

When W. E. Wheeler called that meeting in March 1937, he and those that help to form the club never dreamt that they were giving birth to one of the most prestigious cycling clubs in Wales and indeed Great Britain.

With so much emphasis on the success of the cycling team in the last Olympics, many have turned to this Sport, and so there is one thing that is sure, the Bynea Cycling Club will go from strength to strength in the future thanks to the lads from Bynea.

The only surviving founder member is Mr D. Islwyn Wheeler.

The History group would like to thank the President Mr Tom Samuel for providing us with so much information regarding the present club.

Bynea Cycling club leaving the Clubhouse for club run to Ilston Valley Saturday June 12th 2010.
Left to right: Martin Harsart; Tom Samuel; John Evans (captain) Robert Bennett; Gareth Fenn; Marion Rees.
Front row: John Williams; Paul Rees (vice Captain) Scott Bennett; Edward Laverak.

Origins of the Bynea Cycling Club

The Bynea Cycling Club was started by Willie Wheeler in the middle of 1930. What started as a village cycle group soon became the Bynea Wheeler. There were four others Willie, John, Islwyn and Fred.

During holiday time they would cycle to Porthcawl and spend a week in a large tent. They would cycle to Carmarthen, New Quay and even Lampeter was not beyond them, but then Willie and Islwyn became very good cyclist winning medallists for a number of years. The best cycle track in Wales at that time was in the park in Carmarthen and they would draw huge crowds to see the races.

Many years later they became the Bynea Cycle Club, one of the foremost clubs in Britain with a well known reputation throughout Wales.

There was a story that one of the cyclist also played rugby in the village and at the end of the season, on a trip to Lampeter got quite drunk. On the way home he felt very ill, so the bus stopped outside Lampeter near a field gate, where he proceeded to be sick, When he got home he found that he had lost his false teeth, so he got on his bike and he cycled all the way to Lampeter, retracing his steps, stopping at every field gate until he found them. It was dark when he arrived home saying that he had paid two weeks wages for the teeth and he couldn't afford another set.

Terry Davies 2010

The Champion Cyclist

How proud David Joseph Evans, my father's brother must have been having this photograph taken for winning all these cycling prizes so many years ago. Little did he realise that I his niece would feel equally as proud to own a few.

He lived at Pantyglien, the son of Hannah, daughter of The Butcher's Arms and Joseph, one of 12 children. He emigrated to America, left his precious prizes here with the family. I have cherished letters from him in Philadelphia dated February and May 1921, so he must have had a good few years of cycling experience while keeping a Cycling Shop (census 1901).

Margaret Hannah Davies

LLANELLY
& SOHO HILL BIRMINGHAM

Bynea Rugby Club

Rugby football has always been the major sport in the village of Bynea. Founded in 1883 by Harry Bowen, (headmaster of Bynea School), he was an accomplished player, who had won his first cap for Wales playing against England at St Helen's Swansea on 16th December 1882. By the turn of the last century the rugby team became known as the `Village Boys` and had won recognition in the Llanelli & District, Rugby Union, as well as in the County of Carmarthenshire.

The present Clubhouse at the Butchers Arms and was officially opened in 1967, they celebrated their 125th Year in 2008.

Here are some of those that served on the committee in the earlier days:

A Committee of long ago (c. 1935)
Back Row L/R: Raymond Nicholas, Glyn Morris, Idwal Jenkins, Elvin Withy, George Evans, Dan 'Ponty' Morgan.
Front Row L/R: Cyril Dykes, Dan Roger Thomas, Tom Walters, Ivor Anthony, Cliff Withey.

The Five Caps of Bynea

Over the years Bynea has produced some fine players, there are too many to mention but the following stand out as Bynea has produced 5 Welsh International players:-

Samuel Gethin Thomas
Born in Bynea on the 24.04.1897.
He was a grocer and sub-postmaster Llwynhendy.
Father of Dr Roy Thomas Bynea.
Played for Bynea R.F.C; Llanelli; and Wales.
He gained 4 Caps - England , Scotland, Ireland, France, all in 1923.
He served with the 4th Battalion of the Welsh Regiment in the 1st World War.
Died in Westminster 01.02.1939.

Arthur Bernard Edwards
Born in Station Road, Bynea on the 07.10. 1927, and at the age of 16 years he played for Bynea.
He was educated at Ebbw Vale Grammar School, and attended Aberystwyth and London Universities.
Played for the Army; London Welsh; Llanelli; Ebbw Vale; Swansea; Headingly; Middlesex and Wales.
He was a Full back and gained 2 Caps - Wales against England on 22.01.1955 and against Scotland on 05.02.1955.

Leonard Morris Davies, (Len)
Born on the 30.12.1930.
He was educated at Bynea School; Stradey C. School.
He was employed as a Railway Clerk.
He played for Bynea when he was 16 years old, and also for the Royal Engineers; Kent; and Wales.
He was capped for Wales 3 times - in 1954 against Scotland and France, and 1955 against Ireland.
Len died on the 28.09.1957.

Terence John Davies

(Terry - named in the Welsh Hall of Fame; & made Member of the 'Gorsedd' in the Eisteddfod at Llanelli in 2000. Born in Bynea 24.09.1932. Terry is the brother of Len. He was educated at Bynea School; Stradey C. School. He played for Bynea RFC; Swansea RFC; Devonport Services; Royal Marines; Royal Navy; Devon County; Llanelli RFC; Wales: Barbarians; British Lions. Played as Full back for Wales and gained 21 caps England 6 times; Scotland 5 times; Ireland 3 times; France 5 times Australia once; Played for Swansea v South Africa in December 1951, and was leading scorer.

British Lions v New Zealand 106 points.
Captained Wales 3 times - South Africa 1960; England 1961; and Scotland 1961.
Total points - 7 Convertible Tries; 12 Penalties; 50 Points.
He was the only player to play in 3 Welsh Trials from a 2nd Class Club as Bynea was at the time.

Thomas Kelvyn Coslett

Born in Bynea on the 14.01.1942.
He worked as a Haulage Contractor the Steel works.
Played for Welsh Schools; Welsh Youth; Llanelli; Aberavon; and Wales.
As full back he gained 3 caps v England, Scotland, and France in 1962.
In 1962 he joined St Helen's and scored 4 goals on his debut v Salford on 18.08.1962. He then joined Rochdale Hornets and played for Wales Rugby League. He gained 12 Caps and was also a coach for the Welsh Rugby League.

Won the Lance Todd Trophy (man of steel) in 1972.
Was Inducted into St. Helen's Hall of Fame.
In 2008, he was named as Honorary Life President of the St. Helen's Rugby League Club.

The present day Rugby Club still meet at the Butcher's Arms, and all of Bynea can be proud of the 'village boys' that have brought so much fame to the village.

This plaque was given in memory of Leonard Davies.

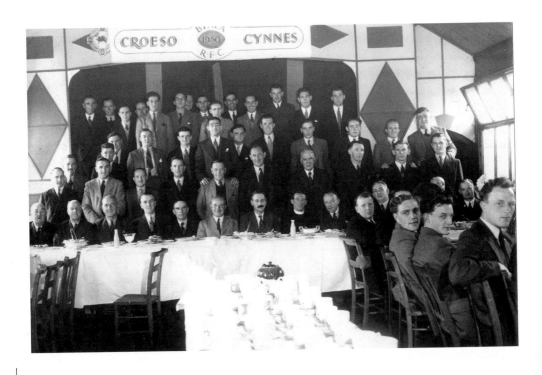

Past Teams

Bynea RFC 1977 - 78
Winners of 'Section D' Shield

Wartime Events
(Taken from Llanelly Mercury
Llwynhendy and District 1939-45)

Throughout the summer of 1939 Britain kept a watchful eye on the events that were unfolding in Europe, and so when Chamberlain announced that 'this country is at war' people did not realise what demands would be made on the 'Home Front'.

The Home Front went to war donning the uniforms, helmets and armbands of their new roles in the Civil Defence, carrying identity cards, and one vital piece of equipment - the gas mask. The carrying of the gas mask would become a matter of routine for everyone, and would have to be checked from time to time.

Even before War was announced the following appeared in the Llanelly Mercury:

Thursday, 31st August 1939
The distribution of gas masks will take place at Llwynhendy council school on Wednesday, Thursday, and Friday evenings of next week; at Bynea School on Wednesday and Thursday and at Bryn School on Friday evening.

Home Guards were also set up. Their headquarters was in the Old School in Llwynhendy.

In 1939/1940 Special Constables were also introduced to the area, in order to help out during the War. One of these was Mr Emrys Dykes, who was a sergeant until he left to serve in the war in July 1942. The following verse was written by one of the special constables, naming those that helped out in Bynea and Llwynhendy.

Special Constables

Y mae Jones y Plismon (Tony Jones) yn slobin o ddyn,
Ei wraig yn un annwyl, y gorau yn y Byd
Mae Victor yr etifedd, un ryfedd yw efe, yn wastad yn roesawus, enwedig amser te
Tony! Tony! Tony! mae'r Jerry yma'n awr, a minnau yn brascamu, ar hyd yr heol fawr.
Mae Morgans yn ddyn distaw, y mae fel hen wch fud, ond hyn a dywedaf, nid ofnaf beth yw'r hyd.
Mae Emrys a mae Meylor yn ddynion pwysig iawn, yn mynd i'r tafarnau i weld bod pethau'n iawn.

APR posts were also set up. The APR wardens patrolled the streets every night for chunks of light showing through every window, and ordinary people were taught to put out fires caused by incendiary bombs, and such demonstrations took places within villages, and towns throughout the war. All this work was done on a voluntary basis.

Thursday 7th September 1939
Will the APR wardens of the district consult the rota which is posted up in the above post?
The 4 posts to be manned as follows:-
1.   *Llwynhendy Old School*
2.   *Gellifach Bryn*
3.   *Fforest Maesarddafen*
4.   *Plough, Bynea.*

Thursday 5th October 1939
To the Editor
Sir,
The Llwynhendy APR Post at the Old School or to give the correct designation
warden s Post No.78 is being manned for the present in the evening only-6-to 10pm.
All the work connected with this is done voluntarily that is to say no pay is being
received.
Rumours are currently that the wardens are well paid some getting 15s. a week.
This is a delusion and it would be well for gossip mongers to pause awhile and not
make such caustic insinuations.
Senior Warden Llwynhendy District.

Much was said during these years about the medals that the troops obtained but also most housewives should have earned a row of them. Theirs was a job and a half and when there was an outside job to do in addition, it was very hard going.

Women went out to work in order to release men for the Forces, and domestic life was completely disrupted during these years. Long queues formed outside shops if it was rumoured that there were tinned food, extra meat, or even other rarities in the shop, thousands of women joined the WVS, that had been started in 1938.

There was a WVS operational in both Bynea and Llwynhendy. In November 1939 Bynea's Comfort Fund had been established to raise funds for those men serving in H. M. Forces in November 1939.

Thursday 11th July 1940
Will those boys joining H.M.Forces residing in Bynea (Loughor Bridge to Soar Chapel) kindly inform Mrs V. Cope Hon.Sec. Bynea Comforts Fund 'Cotswold' Station Road Bynea.

Along with the rest of the Nation the villages of Bynea and Llwynhendy both decided that a house to house collection should be started. By 1941 the WVS and other organisations were in full swing regarding collecting for the Bynea and Llwynhendy Boys.

Thursday 25th July 1940
It is now proposed to make weekly house to house collection of 1d per week and we feel sure that every Bynea household will be glad to have this opportunity of helping in the work of supplying comforts for their own boys.
They held grand variety concerts at the Llwynhendy School and the Recreation Hall in Bynea. Whist Drives were organised and the district Chapels performed their annual concerts. Drama groups put on performances in both Welsh and English and all the money went towards the War Fund.

At the beginning of the war scores of children were evacuated from their homes from the big cities to rural parts, sometimes entire schools were evacuated, along with their mothers and teachers.

Thursday 23rd January 1941
The evacuees of Bynea were entertained to tea organised by the WVS at Bynea Recreation Hall on Tuesday after noon. After the tea Mr Wait of the London County Council addressed the evacuees mothers and children. Others who spoke were Miss German, London; Mrs James teacher of evacuees at Bynea school and Mr James. Expression of thanks were made on behalf of the evacuees by Mrs Temple, and Master David Temple on behalf of the evacuee children. Mrs M.E. Nicholas 'Broadawel' spoke on behalf of the WVS. The following then contributed to an excellent programme - Mrs Sal Thomas, Mrs Fawcett (an evacuee) Miss Mary Vaughan LL.C.M. and Mrs Raynold Nicholas Miss Myra Williams A.T.C.L. was the accompanist.

Thursday 22nd January 1942
The L.CC & Swansea children evacuated to Bynea and their teachers had a very pleasant evening on Tuesday 20th. They enjoyed a scrumptious tea the cost of which was partly born by LCC and the remainder by the WVS. There followed an evening of entertainment, songs and recitations being given by children and games were played.
The evening closed with the singing of the National Anthem.
Many thanks to Mr Isaac Thomas (headmaster) and staff of Bynea school and the WVS for their valuable assistance.

Newspapers were scarce during the war and therefore collection points were set up in both villages so that the villagers could take their used papers for collection.

Thursday 30th May 1940
The waste paper depot at 22 Cwmfelin Row Bynea will henceforth be opened on Monday evenings from 6.30pm and not on Thursday when all waste paper will be gratefully received by collectors.

Thursday 18th June 1942
Please continue to send your book and paper salvage to the official salvage steward Mrs Downing, Aston Villa, Llwynhendy.

As the war went into its 3rd year many of our men were captured and taken as Prisoners of War, and the Red Cross as well as the WVS gave up their time to knit garments for these unfortunate men.

Thursday April 23rd 1942
Last year when Bynea WVS members were knitting for Llanelly House for the British Red Cross POW Parcels Mrs D. T. Nicholas Station Road placed a card in one of the gloves I hope you will have comfort from these also her name and address. Mrs Nicholas has now received a card from Mr Kenneth Steer who is a POW in Germany thanking her and letting her know what a great comfort the gloves had been to him. What better proof could there be that POW do get their parcels.

The years 1939-1945 also brought some of the coldest weather on record, and it lead to teams of women knitting for victory, the WVS of the area were invited by the Llwynhendy WVS to help them.

Thursday 30th July 1942
Our merchants seamen who never fail to bring us our bread and butter are in dire need of woollen comforts especially pullovers. We hope WVS members will be prepared to knit some for them. Wool will be supplied.

Petrol was rationed from the early weeks of war and to ensure a supply for the essential jobs or on war work the use of private cars was banned. In spite of this some found a way of carrying on come what may!

Thursday 18th August 1942
Petrol and travelling restrictions did not affect members of the Bynea Cycling Club during last week, when over 30 members went on tour as far afield as Chester, Colwyn Bay, and Aberystwyth.

Old traditions however still carried on, Soar Chapel held their annual concerts, and Tabernacle held their Eisteddfod, so did the Bynea Eisteddfod carry on as usual.

Thursday 18th January 1940
The Bynea welfare held its Eisteddfod in the recreation Hall on Saturday. It proved a great success and there were numerous entries and apparently the eisteddfod is as popular as ever. The standard reached both in the literary and music sections was extremely high. The committee deserves full credit for the remarkable success of the eisteddfod.

Dydd Nadolig

Dydd Nadolig, dydd i'w gofio
Gorau r holl ddyddiau yw;
Dydd y gnawed Brenin Iesu
Dydd pan unwyd dyn a Duw.
Dydd death Unoedd at eu gilydd
O bellterau daear faith
Gyda chofion am y Ceidwad
i glodfori a'r y death.

Dyma Wyl sy'n para'n newydd
Wedi dwyfil blwyddi maith,
Nid r ysbryd wedi golli
Nid r gan na r aberth chwaith
Dydd Nadolig Llawen seinir
Heddiw fel y dyddiau gynt
Dan y lluoedd a'u anrhegion
Pan y deuant at eu hynt

Ysbryd hael Nadolig annwyl
Aros beirnydd yn ein plith
Cymer feddiant ar y gwledydd
Ymhob calon gwna Dy nyth
Yma dont i garu'i gilydd
Ac ni roddant le i glwy
Fe fydd heddwch fel yr afon
Ac ni ddysgant ryfel mwy.

Penillion gan Joshua Thomas Bynea (buddugol yn Eisteddfod y Bynea 14ed Ionawr 1940.
(verses by Joshua Thomas (winner in the Bynea Eisteddfod 14th January 1940).
(Reported in the Llwynhendy & District Mercury Thursday January 18th 1940).

There was no ending to the ideas that the villagers came up with, and in spite of the hardships and restrictions that they had to face, they also had a great deal of fun.

Rationing had been planned in 1936, and ration books were issued in January 1940. And the wartime population's diet was rich in vegetables and low in sugar and dairy products. Bynea was lucky to receive some 'exotic' fruits by those serving abroad, and in turn they were raffled for the Bynea Comfort Fund.

Thursday 13th May 1943
The lemon sent home from Algiers by Mr Melville Davies was raffled by Mrs M.E. Nicholas and other members of Bynea WVS and realised £7 for the Bynea comforts Fund, the winning number 287.

Thursday 12th April 1945
Bananas and lemons kindly given by Able Seaman Jack Anthony, The Bell, Bynea realised £8 7s 0d for the Comfort Fund.
The women went out collecting fruits to make jam. With rationing in operation lectures were given to the women in both villages regarding jam making.

Thursday 30th October 1941
Mr W. Roadley will be delivering a lecture at Bynea Recreation Hall on Tuesday November 11th 7pm. His subject will be Fruits and Preserving A special invitation is given to the ladies.

Thursday 23rd September 1943
Several members of the Llwynhendy WVS have been busy collecting blackberries and making them into jam. Helped by the Bynea and Llangennech WVS, 150 lbs of jam was sold by the C.W.S. to householders as their jam ration.

Thursday 11th November 1943
The Ministry of Food has commented that the jam made by the Llwynhendy and district WVS was 'of a very high standard and very fruity in flavour'

It was not only the adults that played their part in collecting for the War effort. The youth of both villages also played their part.

Thursday 17th July 1941
Judged by its financial success the Bynea Youth People (The Urdd) movement has more than justified its existence apart from the social amenities provided. During its first 6 months it has reduced the dept on the Recreation Hall by £27 7s 6d while £10. 6s 10d has been spent on the renovation and painting. £15.15s.0d has also been subscribed towards the Bynea Comforts Fund, and besides organising Whist Drives in its aid. They also possess a radiogram to the value of £25. This record is to be highly commended. The chairman is Mr V. Cope, treasurer Nan Griffiths, and Secretary Glanville Jenkins.

Thursday 1st July 1943
Another gift of £1 has been sent to the Red Cross by Gillian and Tony Harries, Audrey Davies and Grace Beynon Bynea gave. It was the proceeds of a jumble sale. The efforts of the children are more than appreciated and thanks are due to Mrs Harries for the help she gave the children in organising it.

Thursday 2nd September 1943
The proceeds of a sale held by 4 Gwelfor boys, Randel Taylor, Roy Charles, John Lucus, and Graham John. The proceeds of a sale held realised the sum of 11s. Handed over to Gwelfor Forces Fund

The most productive campaign was 'Dig for Victory' which saw front gardens used to produce vegetables for the community.

Thursday 3rd April 1941
A meeting of the members of Bynea Horticultural society will be held at Bynea Welfare Pavilion on Tuesday evening next at 6 o' clock. Others are also invited.

Thursday 29th May 1941
Schedules can now be obtained of the Bynea Horticultural Show held on the 9th August. Dig for Victory is the motto of the committee and this show will undoubtedly prove a success.

Thursday 14th August 1941
Bynea Horticultural show at the Recreation hall on Saturday proved a success. Exhibits was of a high standard.

Thursday 28th August 1941
Allotment holders and other interested in gardening are invited to attend a meeting at the Bynea Welfare Pavilion on Friday evening next 7 o' clock for the purpose of forming an organisation to 'Dig for Victory'. Intended members are specially invited as immediate steps should be taken to ensures establishment.

Thursday 4th September 1941
A well attended meeting at Bynea Welfare Pavilion on Friday evening it was decided to form as association to be called 'Bynea Garden & Allotment Association'. Mr Jabez Thomas Gwynfryn was elected chairman, Geraint Thomas treasurer and Mr William Treharne secretary.

In spite of the hard work, the restrictions and the enjoyment the thoughts of the villagers must have been constantly on those who had left their villages to serve in the War. News was constantly being received regarding those who had been wounded, captured or killed, (see the attached 'Role of Honour') but in spite of the separation from relatives and friends, war weary villagers grabbed every opportunity.

During the war the old Pencoed works served as an American Air Force Station, and the strangers soon blended well into the community.

Thursday 14th January 1943
Thoughts of the good old days were brought back to the local sports men last Saturday when rugby was played on the Glynea field. The Bynea RAF Unit has acquired the grounds thanks to the kindness of Mr David Harry J.P. some good open football was witnessed. Local teams who desire fixtures are asked to communicate with the RAF or RFC.

The Chapels have always played a big part in the life of the community and it was no different during the War years. Unlike today the Church and Chapels were the centre of worship as well as everyday life. Their vestries were ever open doors for meetings, drama practises and choirs, all collecting for the same cause.

The wartime government however by the end of 1942 was already looking ahead at the post-war housing and the Beveridge Report on social reform was published.

Thursday December 1942
James Griffiths delivered a very interesting address on the Beveridge Report.

Thursday 4th February 1943
Mr D.R. Grenfell M.P. will be at the vestry at Tabernacle Llwynhendy next Friday at 6.30 pm to speak on 'What kind of New world do we desire?' The Chairman will be W. J. Morgan. A collection will be made.

As the War in Europe came to an end in May 1945 an optimistic note was already growing. Allies celebrated Victory in Europe (V E Day) on the 8th May 1945, and the villagers went ahead to celebrate as all other villages towns and cities in Britain. A meeting was held at Bynea Welfare Pavilion as early as September 1944, and all those who were interested in the forthcoming victory celebrations were invited, and by March 1945 there was a new fund formed by the WVS - Welcome Home Fund

Llanelly Mercury Thursday May 17th 1945
Victory was celebrated in this district by holding street parties, community singing, bonfires etc. and streets gaily flagged. The local schools also had their tea parties.

Llwynhendy and District News, May 17th 1945
Bynea School V.E. celebrations on Friday afternoon commenced with the service of Thanksgiving. The order of the service was the National Anthem; introduction, and a prayer by the headmaster, an address and prayer followed by D. J. Jenkins. (Minister of Soar). 300 children were entertained by Bynea WVS and VE Celebration Committee to a tea including ice-cream. Each child was also given a money gift.
In the evening there were games, sports, and community singing in the school playground.

There were other celebrations also held as the Comfort Fund continued and there was a party given in the June acknowledging the work of the WVS and they were entertained to a tea by the Bynea Victory Celebrations Committee for their good work - now it was known as the Bynea Comforts and Welcome Home Fund.

Slowly the villages settled back to their new way of life -nothing would be as it had been before the War. The single boys returned to their parents, the married ones to their wives and children, but there were many who did not return and their family's loss was felt by both villages, but they were not forgotten, Llwynhendy and Bynea's men had served their country well.

Much has changed since 1945, but the generations that have followed as well as those living in the villages today can say "thank you" to wartime Bynea & Llwynhendy.

Much of the information has been taken from the Llanelly Mercury 1939-1945, 'Llwynhendy & District News', Many thanks to the staff of the Reference Library Llanelli for their help.

Anne Llewelyn (nee Dykes) 2010

Cymdeithasau a Chlybiau
Societies and Clubs
1925-1940

Urdd Gobaith Cymru Fach

Heddiw rydym yn gyfarwydd â chlywed am Eisteddfod yr Urdd a changhennau'r Urdd led led Cymru. Ond tybed faint sy'n ymwybodol fod un o'r canghennau cyntaf o'r Urdd neu – Urdd Gobaith Cymru Fach – fel y gelwir hi ar y cychwyn ym – mhentref y Bynea.

Sefydlwyd adran gyntaf yr Urdd yn y Treuddyn, yn yr hen Sir Fflint yn 1923, ac yna'r adran gyntaf yn y De yn Abercynon Morgannwg yn 1924. Ddim ymhell ar ôl hynny fe sefydlwyd adran y Bynea.

Cafodd yr aelodau gyfle i fynd i'r gwersylloedd cyntaf – Llanuwchllyn, Llangollen, Porthdinllain a'r Wisg Cafodd ambell un o'r pentref gyfle hefyd i deithio tramor. Aeth Vaughan Walters, Penllwyncrwn ar bererindod i Geneva gyda'r Urdd yn 1930.

Roedd yr aelwyd yn cynnal gwahanol weithgareddau ac yn cynnig cyfleoedd amhrisiadwy i'r aelodau. Cynhaliwyd mabolgampau'r Urdd yn Llanelli yn 1932 ac Eisteddfod yr Urdd yn 1939 gydag aelodau'r Urdd o Adran y Bynea yn cymryd rhan.

We are today familiar with the yearly Urdd Eisteddfod and also of its many branches established throughout Wales. Surprisingly enough Bynea was amongst the first of many areas to establish an Urdd branch for its young people. The first branch in North Wales was established in 1923 with the first South Wales branch in Abercynon in 1924. The Bynea branch was established not long after that.

Local members were given the opportunity to visit other areas in Wales while staying at various youth camps in Llanuwchllyn, Porthdinllain, Llangollen and other venues. One of Bynea's young men Vaughan Walters from Penllwyncrwn was given the opportunity to visit Geneva in 1930.

The local branch held various events and gave its members unforgettable opportunities. The annual Sports Day was in Llanelli in 1932 and the Eisteddfod in the Town in 1939 with local youngsters taking part.

Pwyllgor Apêl Llwynhendy, Bynea a'r Bryn, Eisteddfod Genedlaethol Llanelli a'r Cylch 2000

Ym mis Awst 2000 daeth yr Eisteddfod Genedlaethol ar ei thro i fro Llanelli. Ond nid dyma'r dechrau gan fod y bedair blynedd flaenorol wedi bod yn llawn o weithgaredd brwd a diflino gan y pwyllgorau a sefydlwyd ar hyd a lled y Fro gyda'r bwriad o godi digon o arian yn lleol er mwyn sicrhau y byddai'r fenter yn llwyddiant. Roedd gan bob ardal ei phwyllgor gwaith, a'r un sy'n berthnasol i'r hanesyn bach hwn yw – a rhoddi iddo'i iawn deitl swyddogol – Pwyllgor Apêl Llwynhendy, Bynea a'r Bryn, Eisteddfod Genedlaethol Llanelli a'r Cylch 2000.

Cynhaliwyd y cyfarfod cyntaf gyda'r bwriad o ddewis swyddogion yn Neuadd Saron, Bynea gyda Beth Leyshon fel cynrychiolydd o'r Prif Bwyllgor Gwaith yn Llanelli yn llywyddu. Etholwyd Cadeirydd, Ysgrifennydd a Thrysorydd ond ofer fyddai eu henwi yn y fan hon gan i aelodaeth a chyfansoddiad y Pwyllgor newid o bryd i'w gilydd yn ystod y misoedd cyntaf. Yn y pen draw, y prif swyddogion sy'n llawn deilwng o gael eu henwi yw Cerith Owens (Cadeirydd), Alison Owens a Sera Leyshon (Ysgrifenyddion) ac Aelwen Wooldridge (Trysorydd). Fel un a oedd yn aelod o'r pwyllgor rhaid i mi gofnodi inni gael tipyn o hwyl a sbri wrth geisio cael y maen i'r wal yn ein hymdrech i godi arian.

Rhwng 1996 a 2000 cynhaliwyd toreth amrywiol o gyfarfodydd llwyddiannus – rhywbeth at ddant pawb. Mae'r cyngherddau mawr a gynhaliwyd yng Nghapel Nasareth, yn Theatr Elli a Neuadd Pontyberem – a phob tocyn wedi ei werthu – yn dal yn fyw yn y cof. Yfwyd galwyni o de a choffi yn Neuadd Saron ac yn y Ganolfan yn Llwynhendy yn y Boreau a'r Prynhawnau Coffi a The. Cafwyd Nosweithiau Llawen, Helfeydd Trysor, Dawnsio Gwerin a Chasglu o Dŷ i Dŷ. Buom mewn sawl Gwasanaeth Carolau, Cymanfaoedd Canu a Darlithiau ar Emynwyr Cymru a chafwyd portreadau difyr o rannau o nofelau Daniel Owen. I blesio'r merched aethom yn gwmnïau llon i weld pa ddanteithion oedd gan siopau Glyn Ebwy, Casnewydd, Caerdydd a Chaerfaddon i'w cynnig i ni. Cafwyd sawl noson gwis ddifyr yn Nhafarn y Joiners ac yn y Clwb Rygbi yn Bynea. Darparwyd ar gyfer y plant hefyd gyda sawl prynhawn o sbort a sbri yng nghwmni Diamond Dust, Bouncy Castle a Denny Twp – i enwi ond rhai o'r diddanwyr talentog.

Buom yn ffodus iawn i gael gwasanaeth llawer o gantorion, actorion, diddanwyr a chorau
– i gyd yn wynebau yr ydym yn gyfarwydd â nhw ar raglenni teledu Cymru, megis Siân
Cothi, Trebor Edwards, Leah Marion Jones, John Owen Jones, Gillian Elisa, Côr Plant
Hywel, Côr Richard Williams, Côr Ysgol Gyfun Tregwyr a Chôr Meibion Llanelli. Mae
ein dyled iddynt yn fawr. Ar yr un pryd cofiwn a rhown ddiolch i'r cyfoeth o dalentau
lleol a fu mor barod â'u gwasanaeth.

Nid dim ond yr artistiaid sy'n haeddu ein diolch. Ofer fyddai pob cyngerdd, bore coffi
a noson lawen heb gynulleidfaoedd i'w cefnogi trwy werthu a phrynu tocynnau, crasu
dwsinau o bice bach a thorthau o fara brith ar gyfer stondinau gwerthu. Diolch i'r capeli
am eu cefnogaeth, i'r siopau am eu cyfraniadau arian a nwyddau, a'r tafarndai a'r Clwb
Rygbi a'r Ganolfan am eu cefnogaeth o bryd i'w gilydd. Ac o feddwl, efallai mai dyma wir
werth dod â'r Eisteddfod Genedlaethol ar ei thro i'r trefi a'r broydd ar hyd a lled Cymru,
sef rhoi cyfle i'r gymdeithas leol ddod at ei gilydd i gyd weithio a chyd-fwynhau cwmni
ei gilydd.

Do, fe fu'r Eisteddfod yn llwyddiant. Ac unwaith eto, o safbwynt yr hanesyn bach hwn
rhaid dweud mai Pwyllgor Apêl Llwynhendy, Bynea a'r Bryn gododd y geiniog gynta'
ond erbyn y diwedd aeth yr un geiniog honno'n dair mil ar ddeg o bunnoedd (£23,000).

Llwyddiant? Barned y darllenydd.

Louie Saunders

The National Eisteddfod, Llanelli and the area 2000 Llwynhendy, Bynea and Bryn Appeal Committee

In August 2000 the National Eisteddfod of Wales came to Llanelli. This however was not the beginning as the four previous years had been full of fervent and tireless work by the local committee to collect as much funding as possible to ensure the success of the Eisteddfod. Every area had it's own appeal committee and the one that is relevant to this story is that of our own appeal committee- to give it it's official title - Llwynhendy, Bynea and Bryn, Appeals Committee The National Eisteddfod, Llanelli and Area 2000.

The first meeting was held in Saron Hall to elect officials with Beth Leyshon representing the main executive committee in the chair. A chairperson, secretary and treasurer were elected although these changed during the first months, but in the end the main officials were Cerith Owens (Chairman), Alison Owens and Sera Leyshon (Secretaries) and Aelwen Wooldridge (Treasurer). As one of the members of the committee it is worth noting that we all had a great deal of enjoyment whilst endeavouring to fulfill our aim of raising money.

Between 1996 and 2000 a huge variety of events were arranged – something for everyone. The successful concerts that were held in Nasareth Chapel, Theatre Elli, Pontyberem Hall – with every ticket sold – will still be remembered. Gallons of tea and coffee were drunk in Saron Hall and at Llwynhendy Centre on numerous coffee mornings and afternoons. Nosweithiau Llawen, Treasure Hunts, Folk dancing as well as house to house collections were amongst the varied ways the committee strived to reach their goal. We frequented a number of Carol Services, Cymanfa Ganu and interesting talks on Welsh Hymn writers to name but a few events. Day trips were arranged for the ladies to enjoy some retail therapy in Ebbw Vale, Newport, Cardiff and Bath. Enjoyable quiz nights were held at the Joiners Arms and at Bynea Rugby Club. The local children were not forgotten – with many an afternoon of enjoyment with the likes of Diamond Dust, a Bouncy Castle and Denny Twp – to name but a few of the talented entertainers.

We were also very fortunate to have many soloists, actors, entertainers and choirs – all of which were familiar faces on S4C - such as Siân Cothi, Trebor Edwards, Leah Marion Jones, John Owen Jones, Gillian Elisa, Côr Plant Hywel, Richard Williams choir, Côr Ysgol Gyfun Tregwyr and Llanelli. Male Voice Choir. We are indeed indebted to them. However we must also thank and remember the local talent that were so ready to give us their valued time and support.

It is not only the artists that need our thanks. What would every concert , noson lawen and coffee morning have been without an audience to support and assist them – by selling and buying tickets, baking innumerable Welsh Cakes and loaves of Bara Brith to sell on their stalls. Thanks also to the local chapels for their valued support , thanks to the local shops for their donations and to the local public houses and Bynea rugby club and the Centre for their support from time to time. This must be indeed the true worth of having a National Eisteddfod which moves from place to place, from area to area, so that it can provide an opportunity for every local community to pull together, work together and laugh together.

Yes ,the Eisteddfod was a great success .Once again, with regards to this little bit of history , it is possible to say that the Llwynhendy, Bynea and Bryn Appeals Committee collected the first penny, but by the end that little penny became twenty three thousand pounds (£23,000).

A success? You, the reader shall judge.

Louie Saunders

Yr Aelodau cyntaf.

Adran Bynea o Urdd Gobaith Cymru

Eisteddfod Port Talbot.

Eisteddfod Abertawe.

Yn y Gwesylloedd.

Eisteddfod Caerffili.

Hanes yr Eglwys.

Mabogampau Llanelli.

Am dro i Eglwys Fach Talybont.

Eisteddfod Bae Colwyn.

Te Saron.

Yn y Gwesylloedd.

Urdd Play with Ray J. R. Thomas

Drama yr Urdd Adran Bynea a Llwynhendy gyda Ray J. R. Thomas.

Y Blodyn Glâs

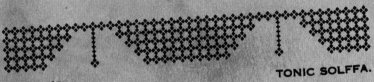

PRIS 1/6.

TONIC SOLFFA.

"Y BLODYN GLÂS"

OPERETA I RAI IEUAINC MEWN DWY ACT

Y Libreto a'r Gerddoriaeth
gan

J. EDDIE PARRY, L.R.A.M.

(Awdur "La Zone," "Cyfrinach y Mor," "Eilunod," etc.)

HUGHES & SON,

Publishers, Wrexham

Eisteddfod Genedlaethol yr Urdd
Llangefni Sir Fôn 1948-49?
Arweinydd: D. Vernon Davies
Cyfeilydd: Moira Wheeler

Pwyllgor Eisteddfod
Bynea, Llwynhendy a'r Bryn

Beth/Sera Leyshon	Bynea
Alison J. Owens	Bynea
Donna White	Bynea
Cerith Owens	Bynea
Byron Williams	Bynea
Ray J. R. Thomas	Llwynhendy
Hettie Davies	Bynea
Thelma Adams	Llwynhendy
Louie Saunders	Bynea
K. V. Roberts	Bynea
Merlys Richards	Bynea
Marilyn Davies	Llwynhendy
Val Beard	Bynea
Len Howell	Llwynhendy
Margaret Howell	Llwynhendy
Moira Lloyd	Llwynhendy
Eirian Davies	Bryn
Irene Thomas	Maesarddafen
Mary Thomas	Pemberton
Ian Woolridge	Bynea
Aelwen Woolridge	Bynea
Eirion John	Llwynhendy
Lynne Davies	Llwynhendy
Michael Bassett	Llwynhendy
D. Cledwyn Bowen	Llwynhendy
Bethan Taylor	Bynea
Menai Morgans	Llwynhendy
Joyce Thomas	Llwynhendy

Swn y Sosban
Perfformiad gan Merched-y-Wawr, Cwmfelin a Bro Cennech, yn Eisteddfod Genedlaethol 2000 yn Llanelli.

EISTEDDFOD 2000
Pwyllgor Apêl
Bynea a Llwynhendy

NOSON LAWEN

yng nghwmni
Cyfeillion Cwmllynfell

**Nos Wener 28 Tachwedd
7.00 p.m.**

Neuadd Saron, Bynea

Pris : £2.50 (oedolion)
£1.50 (plant)

Merched y Wawr, Cwmfelin, Bynea

Sefydlwyd cangen Bynea o Ferched y Wawr ym mis Tachwedd 1996. Ym mis Hydref agorwyd Saron, Neuadd Bentref newydd yng nghanol Bynea, gyda'r bwriad o ddefnyddio'r neuadd i gynnal clybiau a chyfarfodydd amrywiol a fyddai o fudd i bobl yr ardal. Penderfynwyd rhoi cynnig ar gychwyn cangen o Ferched y Wawr.

Cynhaliwyd cyfarfod sefydlu'r gangen ar nos Wener, Tachwedd y 15fed 1996 yn neuadd Saron. Yn bresennol oedd:

Non Griffiths	Trefnydd Cenedlaethol
Val James	Llywydd Cenedlaethol
Betty Thomas	Ysgrifennydd Rhanbarth Myrddin

Roedd chwech ar hugain o ddarpar aelodau yn bresennol hefyd. Aethpwyd ati i ethol swyddogion:

Beth Leyshon	Llywydd
Enid Morgan	Is Lywydd
Sera Leyson	Ysgrifennydd
Bethan Taylor	Is Ysgrifennydd

Penderfynwyd, hefyd,ychwanegu'r enw 'Cwmfelin' at enw'r gangen; hwn yw hen enw ar bentref Bynea ac yn adlewyrchu ceffidir diwydiannol yr ardal.

Bu'r cyfarfodydd ar hyd y blynyddoedd yn gyfrwng pleser i'r aelodau. Roeddent yn amrywio o ran cynnwys a natur gyda'r gwahanol siaradwyr gwâdd. Cafwyd darlithoedd ar iechyd, hobïau, teithio, yr Eisteddfod Genedlaethol (bu'r Archdderwydd a Meistres y Gwisgoedd gyda ni), lleoedd diddorol eu hanes yn yr ardal, arlunio, ffenestri lliw, bagiau llaw, aromatherapy a reflexology ac ati. Cafwyd gwibdeithiau ar hyd a lied de a chanolbarth Cymru a chynhaliwyd sawl parti Nadolig ac, wrth gwrs, cinio Gŵyl Ddewi bob blwyddyn. Ond, daeth tro ar fyd. Ar ôl cyfarfod yn rheolaidd ar nos Lun cynta'r mis am unarddeg o flynyddoedd bu'n rhaid rhoi'r ffidil yn y tô a chau'r gangen ym mis Mehefin 2008. Y rheswm pennaf dros wneud hyn oedd bod nifer yr aelodau wedi gostwng a hynny am y rheswm tristaf, sef colli llawer o aelodau oherwydd salwch a marwolaethau. Ymhlith y chwiorydd a fu farw oedd dwy o'n haelodau ifancaf, sef Marilyn Bassett a Sera Leyshon, a mawr fu'r golled honno. Coffa da amdanynt i gyd.

Merched y Wawr, Cwmfelin, Bynea

In November 1996 the Bynea branch of Merched y Wawr was established . In October, Saron was opened as the New Village Hall in the centre of the village, with the purpose of hosting on the premises, the meetings of various clubs and societies, that would be of benefit to the local residents. Therefore it was agreed to establish the first branch of Merched y Wawr in Bynea.

The inaugurate meeting was held on Friday , 15th November 1996 in Saron Hall.

Those present were:

Non Griffiths	National Organiser
Val James	National President
Betty Thomas	Secretary Myrddin Region

There were twenty six prospective members present. The following were elected as officers:

Beth Leyshon	Chair
Enid Morgan	Vice Chair
Sera Leyson	Secretary
Bethan Taylor	Vice Secretary

It was also agreed to add 'Cwmfelin' to the official title; as this is the old name for the village and reflects the industrial background of the area.

The membership enjoyed rewarding meetings over the years. There were numerous guest speakers who spoke on a variety of subjects. Lectures included health, hobbies, travel, The National Eisteddfod, (the Arch Druid and the Mistress of the Robes being amongst the guests), interesting local historic sites, art, stained glass, aroma therapy, and many others. Trips were arranged in South and Mid Wales , and many a Christmas party was enjoyed, as well as a yearly St David's Day dinner.

Eventually things changed. After meeting regularly for eleven years on the the first Monday of the month it was decided to close the branch in June 2008. The main reason for this decision was that the numbers of members had decreased and the Group became unviable. The membership fell due to the saddest of reasons – illness and death. Amongst those who passed away were two of our youngest members, Marilyn Bassett and Sera Leyshon and great was the loss felt by the branch.

Merched Y Wawr gan Liz Davies.

CROWDS ignore the rain to brouse through the vintage cars show — they had a choice of 80 to inspect.

IGHT acres of Bynea armland sprang to life on aturday at the start of he three - day Celtic estival.

And despite the shock of bad weather the first-ever event ttracted a crowd of 17,000.

"It was a terrific success," enused committee secretary, Mr. eris Edwards.

In fact it was such a winner here may well be a second— ut just when it is too early to ay.

Bynea village became a minia- re Piccadilly, with thousands f cars converging from both lanelli and Swansea.

Police on point duty diverted raffic not going to the festival n to the Bryn road.

But the weather produced a few snags with some of the displays. In the vintage car rally only 80 of the com- petitors turned up instead of the expected 120.

YOUNG potter at the wheel keeps exhibition visitors fascinated.

FESTIVAL BEATS THE MUD SHOCK

ised by a committee set up by St David's Church Llwynhendy ended with an ox-roast and dance organised by Llanelli Lions Club.

Monday was a fairy-tail day for Alsatian Sheba, who was chosen as pet of the day.

For until Mrs. Jenny Smith, of 44, Pengri-road, Loughor, found her in a Llandeilo kennels she hadn't led a very happy life.

When Sheba was brought to the kennels she was in a bad way. She appeared to have been kicked all over and was so thin her bones showed through her skin.

She cowered away from Mrs. Smith but that didn't deter her from taking Sheba home.

And now all the loving care of her new home is beginning to pay dividends.

CIVIC GUESTS

There was no official opening, although the Mayor of Llanelli, Coun. Albert Bowen, went to the festival.

As the rain began organisers were worried that the fields might get muddy.

But only a small dip between two fields proved a problem and they spread duckwalks across it. "I didn't even get my shoes dirty," said one satisfied customer.

One of the highlights was the hilarious Lowland knock- out games. Winners were St. David's Church, Llwynhendy. Runners-up were a team from Bynea Rugby Club.

HEADLAMPS on this gleaming 1909 model get their own plastic macs—but this youngster still finds them worth a closer look.

Heavy rain all over the country made it difficult for the drivers. Some of the cars were oming from as far afield as rimsby.

TRADERS DELAYED

"Some vehicles dated back to 903 and they don't have any oofs—so we can't blame them or not coming," said Mr. dwards.

The Petticoat Lane market aders weren't in full force ither. Many thought the rain ould wash out the festival. thers who decided to come ere held up by floods and idn't arrive until 4 p.m.

But these setbacks didn't dis- earten the organisers—or the pectators. "I can only describe e trade exhibition as fan- stic," said Mr. Edwards, "and veryone enjoyed the pipe and."

One of the surprises of the show was the singing of a party from Bynea C.P. School at Sunday's gymanfa ganu. They accompanied themselves on guitars.

Cor Meibion Llanelli and Cor Henoed rose to their usual andard. Conductors were essrs. Eifion Thomas and Fred rans.

Coun. J. R. Thomas, of Bynea, presided over the hymn festival.

Other highlights of the fes- tival were a concert with Ryan and friends, including Heather Jones, and the Lowland knock- out games.

The event, which was organ-

CARVING out the portions at the Lions Club ox-roast is President, Mr. John Thomas. The meat had been on its spit over a coal fire all day.

Bynea Cycling Club staged a 75-mile road race for those of us who favour two-wheeled transport. The Port Talbot club swept the field.

Result: 1, J. Davies, Port Talbot; 2, K. Sparks, Port Talbot; 3, C. Sparks.

A prize was also given for the child on the field with the best decorated bicycle. Result: 1, Louise Jones; 2, Amanda Jones; 3. Simon Thomas.

The trade exhibition which acted as background to the events included stands show- ing caravanning, sailing and camping, pottery, photography, art and many other items.

Festival was organised by a committee from St. David's Church, Llwynhendy. Proceeds will go to local charities.

GIRLS from Bynea C.P. School join in the hymns in the gymanfa ganu under canvas.
Starpix: Brian Watkins.

SCENES FROM THE CELTIC FESTIVAL

Ryan Davies, who opened the Celtic Festival.

Heather Jones, one of the artists appearing at the Celtic Festival.

Members of the audience trying their hand (or rather feet) at Clog Dancing. They are Dr. Roland Hughes of Llwynhendy and Mel Tonge.

Bynea C.P.School at the Celtic Festival.

The Ray Williams stand at the Celtic Festival.

The Brewers stand at the Celtic Festival.

158

Happy Days!

'Village Trip 1927'

What a good looking group. Note speed limit of Charabanc 20 m.p.h.!! Did they ever get here or there? Iestyn Edwards - back seat wearing sunglasses, Maelgwyn Edwards - next to back door wearing a flower, Gwynfor Owen - centre door wearing a cap.

Parc Gitto - Hendre Road and Erw Las, 1947.

Festival of Britain Carnival, Llwynhendy, 1951.

Llwynhendy Carnival 1950
St. David's Church on the right.

Rhai o blant Ysgol Brynsierfel - 1968?
Some of the pupils of Brynsierfel School - 1968?

Bynea and Llwynhendy Carnival - May 1989
St David's church - entering into the spirit of things !!! Oh-La-La`

Hŵyl a Sbri gyda Côr Meibion Cwmfelin 1964/65 arweinydd Denver Phillips.
Fun and laughter with Cwmfelin Male Voice and their conductor Denver Phillips

Happy Memories of Village Tradition

Many years ago it was the custom for young boys of all ages to sing Calenning from door to door on New Years' Day.

The words of the song would go, as follows:-
Calennig, calennig, bore dydd y calan
Nawr mae'r amser i rhanu'r arian.
Blwyddyn newydd dda i chwi
Ac i bawb sydd yn y tŷ.
Dyma yw'n nymuniad i,
Casglu at y flwyddyn hon.

I wish you a Merry Christmas,
'A Happy New Year'
A pocket full of money
And a cellar full of beer.
The roads are very dirty,
My shoes are very clean,
I've got a little pocket to put my penny in.
If you haven't got a penny,
A halfpenny will do.
If you haven't got a halfpenny
God bless you.

O byddwch môr garedig i agor drws y tŷ,
Mae'r flwyddyn mwyaf lwcis
Yn dyfod atoch chwi
Blwyddyn newydd dda Mr a Mrs Thomas a'r teulu i gyd.

This day was the highlight of the Christmas season in the minds of boys, for it started with an early rise, enthusiastic washing, hair brushing and vigorous cleaning of teeth. All bright and shining, dressed in cap, navy belted mackintosh, bare knees, short trousers and a sturdy pair of shoes.

Roland would go out to meet his pals, Alun Job and David Bennison. It was not policy to be more than three boys, no girls allowed, for it was considered lucky to see a dark-haired male first on New Year's Day.

The three of them would hurriedly go to the home of Mr and Mrs Rees Thomas, which adjoined our garden and lustily sing Calennig. With hot breath steaming in the cold morning air, they would then run to Mr and Mrs Gethin Thomas, the local Post-Office. It did not matter that they had just met Roy, their son, running in the opposite direction with his pals. On that day, housewives set aside the morning for the task of opening the door to singers.

After much running and singing, breath became short and the words indistinct, one demanding housewife would insist that the boys should repeat the song. Another cautious mother, when she saw the 'Doctor's son', would retreat to fetch an extra shilling, to keep 'well-in' with the Doctor.

It always amazed me, how clever the boys were to apportion out their correct share on route. Holes in pockets had to be guarded against.

At twelve-o-clock midday sharp, all singing ceased, the highlight of the day began, a free ride on the trolley-bus which ran from Loughor to Llanelly. On one occasion, Roland arrived home with a bulge above the belt of his mackintosh where he was carrying a willow-pattern jug, a present for me bought at Woolworths for sixpence. The jug is still one of my greatest possessions. Another time he bought 1 lb of Radiance toffees, with his money, resulted in him being violently sick.

I should like to recall after thirty years of dedicated and devoted service, both night and day, at Llwynhendy Health Clinic the work of 'Roland and Roy' (but always 'Doctor' to their faces). Sadly Roland, my son, is no longer with us, but our best wishes go out to Roy for a long and happy retirement.

This story was written by Mrs E. M. Hughes (late of Bwlch Farm).

Diwedd y Daith

Diolch yn awr i'r cyfranwyr –
Eu lluniau ,a'u hanesion di- ri,
A diolch am bob tamaid o gymorth
A wna'r llyfryn yn fyw i ni.

Y nod oedd ceisio cloriannu
Digwyddiadau cofiadwy i chwi,
Am bob math o wahanol fudiadau,
Fu'n ffynnu'n ein hardal ni.

Ceir sôn am y corau a'u doniau,
Am gyngherddau amrywiol eu naws,
Am glybiau a chymdeithasau,
A wna bywyd pob dydd yn haws.

Rhyw bwtyn go fyr sydd yma
Yn cloriannu'r atgofion a fu –
Felly mwynhewch y pori a'r darllen
Maen nhw am eich perthnasau chwi.

Mae bywyd Llwynhendy a'r Bynea
Wedi newid yn fawr , welwch chi,
Ond mae'n bosib i ni hel atgofion
-Am gyfoeth y bywyd a fu.

H.L.